T0339540

Age of Agency

"When the digital world started, many companies moved slowly and cautiously, not willing to replace their traditional operations. Now most companies have gone digital. We are now moving beyond digital into an AI world. Don't ignore it. This important book will guide you by providing a fresh perspective on the interrelationships between humans and AI."

– Philip Kotler

Do you feel overwhelmed by the AI wave? Worried that it could cost you your job, harm your business, or even take over?

AI has pervaded our lives and is aggressively disrupting business. No person today can afford to ignore AI.

Age of Agency: Rise with AI is your companion, helping you leverage AI's capabilities to power your productivity and success. By understanding AI, you will learn to use it as a tool for personal career growth and business success.

Former Microsoft executive Kerushan Govender demystifies AI, emphasising the importance of human agency, reconnecting with the needs of humanity and learning the importance of care as a differentiator in an AI world to avoid the potential pitfalls of excessive reliance on the technology.

This book is a blueprint for ensuring human agency outpaces computer agency. It boldly pits the limits of machine learning against the infinity of human ability. With this survival guide, you'll uncover ways to connect with humanity on a deeper level, going beyond anything AI can do.

Ready to become AI-savvy with your humanity as your differentiator? Dive into the future with the confidence to ride the wave of today's AI revolution.

Kerushan Govender merges scientific expertise with real-world business acumen. He boasts a flair for technology, from teaching coding decades ago to more recent leadership roles at Microsoft. He serves on the Board of the American Marketing Association, New York City chapter, and sits on an Advisory Board of the University of Cape Town. Kerushan's work resonates with those seeking a transformative shift in their careers and business. Visit kerushan.com to learn more.

Age of Agency

Rise with AI

Kerushan Govender

Routledge
Taylor & Francis Group
A PRODUCTIVITY PRESS BOOK

First published 2024
by Routledge
605 Third Avenue, New York, NY 10158

and by Routledge
4 Park Square, Milton Park, Abingdon, Oxon, OX14 4RN

Routledge is an imprint of the Taylor & Francis Group, an informa business

ISBN: 978-1-032-68488-8 (hbk)
ISBN: 978-1-032-68486-4 (pbk)
ISBN: 978-1-032-68489-5 (ebk)

DOI: 10.4324/9781032684895

Typeset in Garamond
by Deanta Global Publishing Services, Chennai, India

Dedication
In loving memory of my mom.
I was always prouder of you than you knew.

Contents

SECTION 2 MASTER AI

SECTION 3 DEVELOP CARE

SECTION 4   UNDERSTAND HUMANITY

Preface

The tidal wave of artificial intelligence (AI) has arrived, reshaping the landscapes of industries, businesses, and personal lives globally. Are you a business owner, a team leader, a budding entrepreneur, or perhaps an individual seeking to ride this wave rather than being swept under? If so, this book is for you. In the *Age of Agency: Rise with AI*, we offer you a compass, a guide, as you navigate the sometimes treacherous, often confusing, but undeniably exciting terrain that marks the onset of this new era.

In this digitally dominant landscape, perhaps you ask important questions: How can I leverage AI without losing the human touch? How do I embrace this technological innovation while still maintaining and enhancing my agency? How do I ensure that my business thrives in this AI era without losing its soul, human connection, and empathy? You are not alone in these contemplations.

As a business owner, you may be grappling with the shift in business dynamics. The challenges of integrating AI technology into your operations, training your workforce to adapt to this new reality, and ensuring that your products and services remain relevant and appealing to a rapidly evolving customer base are real and pressing issues.

As a team leader, the human–computer interplay might be throwing up unique challenges for you. You might be wrestling with the puzzle of ensuring your team members work harmoniously with AI tools while nurturing their own unique human abilities. The balancing act of exploiting AI's efficiency and fostering your team's creativity, intuition, and emotional intelligence of your team can indeed be daunting.

If you are an entrepreneur in the throes of launching your dream venture in this AI-driven world, you are likely juggling a multitude of considerations. You might be pondering how to position your brand in a market increasingly defined by algorithms and data, foster genuine connections with your customers in a virtual environment, or leverage AI without losing sight of your human-centric vision.

For individuals, the questions may be even more existential. Will I be rendered irrelevant by AI? How can I upskill or reskill to ensure relevance in the job market? How do I maintain my agency, decision-making power, and creativity in a world increasingly dominated by machines?

This book speaks directly to all these pain points. The *Age of Agency: Rise with AI* is your survival guide and your growth manual rolled into one. It is your handbook for maintaining your relevance, human agency, and capacity for genuine care and empathy in an age characterized by AI dominance. It is your guidebook for rising, not just surviving, in the AI era.

Let's be clear. This book is not just another discourse on the rise of AI and the impending doom of human irrelevance. Far from it. At its core, this book is about empowerment, resilience, and the celebration of human agency. It is about harnessing AI as a tool, not viewing it as a threat. It's about embracing AI as a tool, not a competitor. It's about redefining the narrative of AI from a fear-inducing disruptor to an opportunity-laden facilitator.

In the *Age of Agency: Rise with AI*, we explore the depths of personal agency, the power of human potential, the impact of genuine care, and the significance of effective positioning. The insights shared here come from years of meticulous observation, deep enquiry, and thoughtful analysis. We delve into examples, real-world applications, and practical strategies to give you a robust understanding and a clear path forward.

This is a critical read for all those who wish to thrive in the new era, who refuse to be passive spectators and instead choose to be active participants, harnessing the power of AI to fuel their dreams and aspirations. The stakes are high, and so are the opportunities. Welcome to the *Age of Agency: Rise with AI*. Buckle up for an enlightening journey into the uncharted territory of the AI era, armed with the powerful tools of human agency and empathy.

About the Author

Kerushan Govender is a leading figure in the business and technology world, revered for his ability to craft and execute transformative strategies. His business acumen, paired with his deep understanding of technology and culture, has positioned him as a key authority on organizational efficiency, growth, and digital transformation.

As the CEO of Blacfox, a renowned marketing strategy consultancy that serves industry giants like Microsoft, SAP, and VMware, Kerushan brings a unique blend of business growth expertise, marketing prowess, and cultural stewardship to the table. His role at Blacfox involves crafting customer acquisition and retention strategies for some of the world's largest brands and shaping the narrative around their offerings, a role that he is eminently qualified for.

Before his tenure at Blacfox, Kerushan spent a decade in leadership roles at Microsoft. There, he was instrumental in doubling a $250M segment that spanned over 80 countries in just three years. He also transformed a $10M business into a thriving venture with an annual turnover of more than $50M in under three years.

Kerushan's media appearances further reflect his authority on business, technology, and culture. Notably, he has appeared on WFLA's Daytime show, where he provided insights on "Technology with a Human Touch." His views are widely respected, and his ability to communicate complex ideas in a relatable way makes him a valuable source of knowledge and inspiration.

This vast array of experiences, credentials, and accomplishments make Kerushan an ideal author for this book. His approach to strategic thinking, culture, and technology, combined with his dedication to high-agency societies, form the backbone of his writing. His ability to draw on his extensive professional background to deliver insightful, practical, and engaging content uniquely positions him to write a book that will resonate with readers and make a meaningful impact on businesses and societies.

Chapter 1

Introduction

The Concept of Agency

This book centres on the concept of "agency" – the capacity of individuals or teams to act independently and make their own free choices. It recognizes the profound power within individuals, equipping them with the knowledge, skills, and confidence to make decisions, take initiative, and be accountable for their actions.

High-agency culture is introduced as a vital aspect of progressive organizations where employees actively shape their work environment and contribute to organizational goals. These individuals are problem-solvers, confident in overcoming obstacles, innovating, and driving growth.

In this high-agency culture, human resourcefulness and creativity are critical enablers of progress and innovation. It's here that agency, creativity, and resourcefulness intertwine, forming a dynamic trinity that empowers individuals to think outside the box, find innovative solutions to complex challenges, and ultimately, shape their destinies.

An essential narrative that we uphold throughout this book is that AI, while an impressive technological feat, remains but a tool. A tool that can augment human capabilities, not replace them. By performing routine tasks, offering data-driven insights, and supporting decision-making, AI can free humans to focus on areas we excel in: strategic thinking, creativity, and interpersonal connections. It does not supersede human agency, but rather, it magnifies it. It helps individuals to achieve their potential, consequently contributing to organizational growth.

This era is rightfully dubbed the Age of Agency. Not because of the rise of some illusionary concept of "computer agency" but because it is when human agency must be at its most potent. The term "computer agency" is sometimes used to represent the capacity of AI systems to act autonomously, make decisions, and execute tasks without human intervention. It paints an image of AI systems transitioning from mere tools to independent agents.

However, this representation is a mirage. A seductive illusion. While AI systems can learn, adapt, and make predictions or recommendations based on data, they remain wholly dependent on human input and guidance. They operate within the constraints defined by their human creators. AI does not possess its own agency but rather augments human agency.

This book seeks to clarify these concepts, dispelling the myth of computer agency while highlighting human agency's real and profound power. It navigates the delicate interplay between humans and their tools in this Age of Agency, illustrating how AI can be harnessed effectively to enhance human agency and drive growth and innovation that upholds human values and fosters a high-agency culture.

In its essence, this book posits that the real power in this Age of Agency remains with us, the humans. This age is ours. This is our time to assert our agency and shape our future. This is the Age of Human Agency.

Connecting the Dots

Age of Agency: Rise with AI isn't merely a call to action – it's an ultimatum. With the Age of AI no longer on the horizon but reshaping the very fabric of our lives and careers, we must either embrace and ride this wave or risk being washed away. The prevailing sentiment in the market is one of trepidation. The unknown magnitude of AI's implications – what it signifies for individuals, teams, and entire organizations – is daunting.

To quell this fear, Part 1 of the book emphasizes our unparalleled human potential. In the face of AI's imposing stature, our innate faculties of observation, creativity, and resourcefulness stand unchallenged. This grounding realization not only soothes apprehensions but also sharpens our understanding of which capabilities we need to hone, bet on, and showcase more prominently, ensuring we always feel empowered rather than threatened by AI.

Then, Part 2 prompts us to shift our lens and view AI not as an adversary but an ally. By mastering its nuances and capabilities, we can delegate the routine and amplify our efforts on tasks that truly matter. The onus is on us: understand AI's abilities and limitations, and instead of being subjugated by it, channel its potential to bolster our endeavours.

Transitioning from the personal realm, Part 3 casts its gaze on the world of customer interactions. In this AI-dominant era, genuine care in transactions is not a vestige of the past; it's the game-changer of the future. As AI refines operational efficiencies, our differentiator lies in infusing humanity into every transaction, ensuring every digital touchpoint reflects authentic care, fostering trust and loyalty.

In Part 4, the emphasis is on the importance of retaining our humanity in a market burgeoning with AI-generated content. Despite the digital inundation, we must never lose sight of the tangible world where real people seek real value. It's essential to constantly reconnect with what truly matters, reminding ourselves of the core reasons behind our actions. This remains a world driven by human needs and desires; our positioning should reflect that. While AI may amplify our reach, our value proposition should be deeply rooted in human-centric service. Now, more than ever, it's vital to stay anchored in this truth.

As the AI tidal wave surges, it's our unrelenting human spirit that will ensure we rise. Equipped with the insights from these pages, the time to act is now — because in this new era, only inaction spells true peril.

Ready for Lift-Off?

Imagine standing at the helm of an advanced, state-of-the-art aircraft, ready for take-off. The cockpit is brimming with advanced instrumentation and automated systems designed to make flying a breeze. Among these, the autopilot is particularly enticing – a system capable of controlling the aircraft's trajectory, so you don't have to. But despite all this technology, you, the pilot, are charged with ensuring the safe and successful journey of the plane and its passengers.

The world of AI is much like piloting this aircraft. AI is the autopilot – sophisticated and powerful. You are the pilot – skilled, vigilant, and in command. Much like an autopilot, AI can relieve you of the mundane and the tedious, but it is not autonomous in the truest sense. It requires your oversight, your judgement, and your human touch. Just as pilots are needed to take critical decisions in the face of the unexpected, to communicate with air traffic control and passengers, and to steer the aircraft safely through storms, you, as the AI pilot, are needed to guide AI through the complexities of human life and society.

A pilot sets the course for the destination. Similarly, with AI, setting the right objectives and goals is essential. AI is exceptionally good at optimizing and finding the best routes to achieve a target. However, defining that target, understanding its implications, and ensuring it aligns with human values and ethics is a task only a human can undertake. As an AI pilot, you are responsible for ensuring that AI's course is not only efficient but also ethical and humane.

Every flight may encounter unexpected turbulence. A human pilot is trained to stay calm, assess the situation, and take appropriate actions to ensure safety. In AI, turbulence can take the form of unpredictable market changes, ethical dilemmas, or algorithmic biases. As an AI pilot, your human judgement, intuition, and ability to think beyond data are indispensable in navigating these challenges.

Pilots are often commended for smooth landings; it is a delicate art that requires precision and finesse. In the context of AI, a landing can be likened to the successful implementation and integration of an AI system within society. It requires ensuring that the AI system does not inadvertently harm or marginalize any group and that its benefits are accessible to all. It requires a human touch, an understanding of human values, and a commitment to serving humanity.

A pilot communicates continuously with the control tower, ground staff, and passengers. As an AI pilot, maintaining open communication channels with stakeholders, customers, and the community is crucial. This involves listening to feedback, understanding concerns, and being transparent about the capabilities and limitations of AI systems.

Interestingly, despite the advancements in aviation technology, there has never been a serious discourse suggesting that pilots have become obsolete. The capable technology of a modern aircraft is not seen as a competitor to the pilot; rather, it's an ensemble of tools at the pilot's disposal. This is a powerful and instructive paradigm. The relationship between a pilot and the aircraft's technology is one of harmony and command.

The pilot, with human judgement, experience, and accountability, is the orchestrator of this technological symphony. The technology augments the pilot's capabilities but never takes away the pilot's authority or responsibility. As an AI pilot, embracing a similar harmony is key. The AI technologies are your instruments, and you are the maestro conducting them. They are there to empower you, but they do not usurp your place at the helm. Your command is quintessential and irreplaceable.

In *Age of Agency: Rise with AI* being an AI pilot means harnessing the power of AI but never letting go of the controls completely. It's about rising with AI, steering it in a direction that reflects our collective values, and ensuring a safe and inclusive journey for all humanity. As you read through the parts of this book, you'll be equipped with the insights and tools needed to be an adept pilot in the AI age, able to take off, navigate, and land with the precision and care that only a human can provide. Buckle up, and get ready for lift-off.

MASTER YOUR OWN AGENCY

1

At the helm of thriving in the artificial intelligence (AI) age is the mastery of your own agency. This part is a deep dive into fortifying your innate human faculties – observation, resourcefulness, and creativity. These human traits become your unparalleled edge in a world progressively reliant on AI. Why is this critical? As AI systems take on more tasks, it's easy to become complacent. But complacency is the underbelly of stagnation. To be indispensable in this AI era, you must sharpen these human faculties to see what AI can't, innovate where it's rigid, and adapt where it falters. This is about being proactive rather than reactive, about charting the course instead of drifting in the current. Harness your inherent human agency and set the foundation for unyielding growth.

DOI: 10.4324/9781032684895-2

Chapter 2

Defining Agency

Unleashing Human Potential

In the vast and rapidly evolving field of AI, it's easy to be overwhelmed by the extraordinary capabilities that these systems seemingly possess. AI appears to be an undeniable game changer from predictive analytics to autonomous vehicles. However, amidst the awe and fascination, we must firmly grasp an essential truth: the capabilities of AI are not on par with human potential, not even close.

In its current form, AI is a tool, an instrument, and a means to an end. It is proficient at specific, well-defined tasks, processing data at a speed no human can match. However, it fundamentally lacks the nuanced understanding, creativity, empathy, and wisdom that define our human nature. These are the realms where humans triumph, the domains where we excel, and these unique human capabilities must be emphasized.

It is not a power play between humans and AI, for there is no real competition. To suggest such a contest is to wrongly equate a tool, albeit powerful, with its user. Human potential is boundless; it dwarfs any capability AI has or ever will have. We must not blur this distinction.

The aim is not to suppress AI but to harness it to enhance human potential and create a synergy between human creativity and AI's computational power. However, a careless or overzealous adoption of AI can lead to alienation. If AI takes over tasks without a thoughtful approach, we risk creating systems that lack the human touch. For example, AI chatbots can offer speedy responses in customer service but often miss subtleties in customer sentiment, leading to dissatisfaction. This isn't a failure of AI failure; it's a testament to the complexity

DOI: 10.4324/9781032684895-3

7

and depth of human communication, demonstrating our unique capacity for empathy and understanding.

We need to wisely discern where and how to integrate AI so that it supports, not replaces, human capabilities. Consider the case of retail security systems: AI is used to detect checkout scanning errors in retail stores, not because humans are incapable of such detection, but because it is a tedious, rule-based task that no human should have to endure. AI takes over this repetitive job, freeing humans to engage in more meaningful and fulfilling tasks.

The discourse around AI should be democratized, including all stakeholders. Decisions about AI should not be left to tech companies or detached policymakers alone but should involve those it affects. In doing this, we ensure that AI is designed and used in a way that truly serves humanity.

As we marvel at what AI can do, let's not lose sight of the extraordinary capabilities we possess as humans. Let's shift the discourse from a false competition with AI to celebrating human potential. The goal of AI should not be to surpass humans but to serve and enhance our capabilities. The future of AI should be human-centric, harnessing the strengths of AI to amplify our innate capabilities. Only by doing so can we ensure that AI serves us, not the other way around.

ChatGPT, developed by OpenAI, represents one of the most impressive advances in AI. This language model generates human-like texts, often producing responses that closely resemble what a human might say. However, despite its sophistication, it's important to remember that ChatGPT is far from matching the full spectrum of human capabilities.

One of the core limitations of ChatGPT lies in its understanding of context. While being capable of processing text and generating responses based on patterns learned during training, ChatGPT cannot truly comprehend context the way humans do. It doesn't have a consciousness or personal experiences to draw upon, and complex emotions or cultural nuances inherent in human communication are beyond its grasp. When it appears to display understanding, it's merely producing a response based on the patterns in the data it was trained on.

In addition, ChatGPT's knowledge is static, with a cut-off point (September 2021). It can't update its understanding with new information or developments unless it's retrained with new data. This means it can provide outdated or incorrect information and even struggle with providing the correct date.

ChatGPT cannot also critically evaluate its responses or learn from its mistakes in real-time, a characteristic common to humans. Despite its impressive consistency in producing results without fatigue or loss of focus, this strength can also be a weakness. It will consistently produce outputs based on the patterns it has learned, even when those patterns lead to incorrect or nonsensical responses.

Furthermore, ChatGPT, like all AI, has no agency or intent. Despite its ability to generate seemingly meaningful text, it doesn't have desires, beliefs, or goals and doesn't understand the implications of its responses. It's a tool to aid human capabilities, not replace them.

The true value of AI lies not in outperforming humans but in complementing our abilities. Even an unmotivated or disengaged human possesses a depth of understanding, creativity, and contextual awareness that far outstrips the most advanced AI. The seeming brilliance of ChatGPT is predicated on vast amounts of data and computational power, yet it still lacks the basic human abilities of common-sense reasoning, true understanding, and real-time learning. It can produce impressive responses based on patterns but can't interpret or understand those responses in a truly human sense.

It's crucial to remember that AI is a powerful tool, but a tool, nonetheless. AI should be used to take over monotonous tasks and provide analytical prowess, freeing humans to focus on tasks that require creativity, empathy, strategic thinking, and the uniquely human touch. The goal is and always should be human-centric AI.

In the face of the hype surrounding AI technology, we must not overlook its limitations. A profound respect and acknowledgement of our innate human capabilities should temper the excitement. As we continue advancing AI technology, we should celebrate the irreplaceable depth and richness of human potential and ensure that the focus remains on enhancing human potential, rather than the illusory pursuit of surpassing it. AI should be a partner, not a competitor, and the future of AI lies in its ability to augment human potential, not in futile attempts to replicate or surpass it.

AI is a powerful, transformative tool, yes – but a tool nonetheless. And as with any tool, its efficacy lies in its wielder's hands. This fundamental understanding paves the way for a significant paradigm shift in our approach to AI: moving from restriction to empowerment.

In the early days of AI, much of the discourse was centred around constraining its potential, fearing that unchecked advancements might lead to a dystopian world where machines outperform humans in nearly every aspect. This led to debates about creating "AI-proof" jobs or imposing regulatory restrictions on AI capabilities. While these concerns are valid, they stem from an adversarial perspective that views AI as a potential threat rather than a tool.

However, the real power of AI lies in its ability to augment human capabilities, not replace them. Rather than focusing on building barriers around AI, we should look at how we can harness its power to solve complex problems, drive innovation, and improve lives.

Consider, for instance, the way AI can transform healthcare. By analysing large amounts of data quickly and accurately, AI can help identify patterns that would be impossible for humans to discern. This doesn't render doctors obsolete; instead, it empowers them with actionable insights, enabling them to make better-informed decisions about patient care.

In this new age of AI, we face a unique challenge and opportunity: to outperform not just our past selves but the tools we have created. This is the era of the Age of Agency, a time where the "average" is constantly being redefined by the capabilities of AI. However, amidst this sea of "average," we must remember that humans have an inherent capacity for growth, improvement, and excellence. We must strive to be more than just users of advanced tools; we must aim to be architects of our own destiny and masters of these tools.

AI is not just forcing us to compete; it's compelling us to evolve. The urgency to outshine yesterday's best has never been more pressing. In the wake of AI's vast potential, we are reminded of our untapped reservoirs of creativity, innovation, and empathy. The real value of AI doesn't just lie in its capacity to empower us but also in its ability to mirror our potential, to push us towards becoming the best versions of ourselves.

In this transformative journey, AI serves as both a magnifying glass and a mirror: it amplifies our abilities while reflecting who we are and who we can be. By harnessing the power of AI, we can transcend the "average" and strive for excellence. This is not just about leveraging AI; it's about raising the bar of human capability.

But it's crucial to remember that this isn't a passive process. We must actively engage with this challenge, confront the reality of the Age of Agency, and understand that in this new landscape, complacency is not an option. We need to continuously strive for improvement, push the boundaries of what's possible, and be better than we were yesterday. This is the true promise of AI: to catalyse human growth and be a testament to our potential for continual evolution.

But how do we facilitate this paradigm shift? It begins with education. By demystifying AI and helping people understand its potential, we can shift the conversation. Instead of discussing how to restrict AI, we can discuss empowering individuals to leverage AI effectively.

We also need to build trust in AI systems. This involves creating transparent and explainable AI that users can understand and interact with. By giving people insight into how AI makes decisions, we can help them feel more comfortable using it.

We need to create frameworks and policies that encourage responsible AI use. This means ensuring that AI systems are fair, accountable, and designed with user-centric principles in mind. By creating guidelines prioritizing human autonomy and decision-making, we can ensure that AI is used as a tool for empowerment, not subjugation.

Embracing this paradigm shift means recognizing the immense potential of AI while acknowledging its limitations. It means using AI to extend our abilities, not to constrain them. By shifting our focus from restriction to empowerment, we can harness the power of AI in a way that truly benefits humanity. After all, the value of AI doesn't lie in its ability to mimic human behaviour but in its capacity to empower us to achieve more than we could alone.

But more than that, the emergence of AI challenges us to rise above our limitations and continually strive for excellence in a world where "average" is no longer good enough. AI is not just a tool for improvement; it's a call to action, a demand for us to be better, push the boundaries of our capabilities, and strive for continuous growth. The era of AI is not just about machine learning; it's about human learning and evolving, too.

In the Age of Agency, the narrative must not omit the urgent need for us to improve as a humanity. Yes, AI is forcing us to be better. But it also serves as a stark reminder that we humans have the capability and responsibility to keep improving. In a sea of "average" brought to bear by AI, we must become those shining examples of human excellence. Now, more than ever, we need to shine, whether we like it or not. The pressure to be better than yesterday has never been more urgent. AI is not the end of our journey; it's the beginning of a new chapter in our evolution – one that we write ourselves.

In the face of rapid technological advances, particularly in AI, it is crucial to strategize how best to uphold and strengthen human agency. At this pivotal moment in history, the objective should be to leverage the development and application of AI to augment human capabilities, not to erode human autonomy.

Foremost among these strategies is education. A well-informed society is the foundation of any strategy to bolster human agency. Understanding AI needs to become commonplace, extending beyond technological circles and infiltrating schools, businesses, and government organizations. This goes beyond understanding the technical aspects of AI – it includes grappling with ethical considerations, potential benefits, and inherent risks.

Individuals and organizations alike need to prioritize digital literacy and continuous learning. In an era increasingly shaped by AI, it is essential to equip people with the skills necessary to understand, navigate, and influence these new systems. Digital literacy extends beyond basic computer skills – it encompasses data analysis, coding, digital marketing, and more. Lifelong learning programmes must be implemented to keep pace with the rapid rate of technological change.

Human-centred design principles should be paramount in AI development. AI systems need to be designed to be transparent, understandable, and controllable by the user. They should augment human decision-making, not undermine it, and allow for human override when necessary.

Rather than focusing on policy changes, society needs to cultivate a greater appreciation for human agency. AI should not be perceived as a means to amplify human capabilities but as a tool to take over mundane and repetitive tasks, freeing humans to engage in activities that AI is fundamentally incapable of performing. This perspective should be the primary narrative.

AI is a tool, not a collaborator. Just as a surgeon uses a scalpel, humans should use AI as a tool. It is a means to an end, not an end in itself.

Amplifying human agency in the age of AI is not a passive endeavour. It requires proactive efforts at individual, organizational, and societal levels. The objective is to ensure that as AI becomes more advanced, we grow in tandem with it, using its potential to empower us rather than allowing it to overshadow or undermine our abilities. As AI evolves, humans should also evolve, using AI as a tool to perform tasks, thus freeing themselves to engage in activities that require uniquely human skills. This is about ensuring that AI is used, not worshipped.

The Power of Personal Agency

In the kaleidoscope of human experiences across cultures, countries, and contexts, the relationship between money and happiness emerges as a compelling narrative, fraught with misconceptions and often overshadowed by societal conditioning. We will dissect, deconstruct, and decode this relationship in this all-important section of the book, inspired by a power-packed workshop that has been delivered with resonating success across the globe.

The workshop, an intense introspective journey that has reverberated in packed auditoriums from Kenya to Dubai, India to Barbados, and the United States to the United Kingdom, serves as a robust foundation for the transformative insights we will unpack here. It has been a catalyst for sparking enlightening dialogues and thought-provoking discussions, breaking barriers of geographical boundaries, and bridging cultural gaps, leading to universal revelations about the intrinsic bond between money and happiness.

Undoubtedly, this is a paramount exercise that will invite you to question ingrained beliefs, challenge accepted norms, and explore a ground-breaking premise that forms the book's bedrock. The insights from this exercise are not just a matter of personal reflection, but they extend to team dynamics and business growth. They serve as a guiding compass, steering you towards a better understanding and appreciation of the pivotal role of personal agency in the unfolding narrative of the Age of Agency.

Let us begin this exploration with a shared understanding that what unfolds in the pages ahead is not a mere academic discourse. It is a transformational journey that you're embarking on, with the potential to reshape your worldview and redefine your approach towards money and happiness.

In the vast panorama of human existence, there are many arenas where money and happiness move in concert, creating a sometimes complex yet undeniably significant relationship. In this section, we will delve into some key areas of this relationship, focusing on the critical role of money in our pursuit of happiness.

First, let's consider education, an aspect of life where money's influence is profound and tangible. Quality education provides a fertile ground for personal growth and intellectual fulfilment, shaping the trajectory of our lives and the lives of our loved ones. It opens up new horizons, broadens perspectives, and seeds the pursuit of a fulfilling career. Yet, the ability to provide this critical asset often comes down to one's financial capability. From private tuition to higher education, money plays a pivotal role in shaping educational opportunities, making its contribution to happiness palpable.

Next, healthcare is another sphere where the relationship between money and happiness is starkly evident. Health is indeed wealth, and money grants us access to a spectrum of healthcare services – preventive measures, cutting-edge treatments, or emergency care. The peace of mind that comes from knowing you have the financial resources to deal with unexpected health crises significantly contributes to overall happiness.

Moving onto the realm of security, another fundamental human need, we see the integral role of financial resources. From residing in a safe neighbourhood to driving a well-maintained vehicle or living in a secure home, the financial means to provide these necessities bestow upon us a sense of safety. This comfort contributes to peace of mind and overall happiness.

Let's not neglect the sphere of small yet meaningful pleasures. The joy derived from a casual coffee outing with a friend, a new book from a favourite author, or a dinner out with family – these seemingly mundane aspects of life add delightful dimensions to our daily existence. However, the ability to afford these experiences is inherently tied to financial means, making money a vital facilitator of such simple pleasures.

In these key areas, we see that money weaves itself into the fabric of our lives, contributing significantly to our happiness. This understanding is not about fostering materialism, but about acknowledging that our financial resources shape our lives, at least in part. This acknowledgement can bring a sense of relief, allowing us to view the pursuit of wealth as an objective, non-judgemental quest, thereby preparing us for the next steps in this exercise.

Having explored the initial facets of the relationship between money and happiness, let's delve further into this dynamic, unfolding more layers of the financial fabric that adorns our lives.

In this modern era, personal fulfilment often comes from pursuing passions or hobbies. From sports to arts, these activities enrich our lives, stimulate our creativity, and provide us with a profound sense of satisfaction. However, pursuing such interests often requires financial investment – a tennis enthusiast requires a racquet and access to a court, and an aspiring painter needs quality brushes and canvases. Therefore, the ability to indulge in these activities to derive joy from them is directly linked to our financial capacity, further emphasizing the role money plays in our happiness.

The next arena to consider is the power of giving and philanthropy. The ability to extend a helping hand to make a positive difference in someone's life can be a deeply fulfilling experience. While altruism isn't solely defined by financial generosity, having the financial resources to aid a friend in need or contribute to a cause close to our hearts undoubtedly adds to our sense of purpose and joy.

Then there's the sphere of capital investment, which is particularly significant for entrepreneurs and business owners. The ability to invest in one's own enterprise to see an idea evolve into a successful venture is not only rewarding but also a major contributor to happiness. However, the launchpad for such endeavours often requires significant capital, underscoring the importance of financial resources.

Lastly, we explore the concept of visibility and networking. In our interconnected world, the ability to forge valuable connections, attend significant events, and establish a strong professional network is critical. It opens doors to opportunities, propels personal and professional growth, and boosts self-esteem. Yet, this visibility often requires financial investment, reinforcing the link between money and happiness.

The relationship between money and happiness is multifaceted, pervasive, and significant. It is not about condoning rampant materialism or propagating the idea that money is the sole key to happiness. Instead, this exploration helps us to acknowledge the undeniable role of financial resources in facilitating various aspects of our lives, contributing to our overall sense of fulfilment and contentment. It is about liberating us from the guilt often associated with pursuing financial stability, making it a legitimate, integral part of our quest for a fulfilling life. This acceptance prepares us for the next steps in our journey, embracing the powerful role of resourcefulness in creating the life we desire.

As we progress through this introspective exercise, let us shift our focus to the vast landscape of human experiences that evoke profound happiness independent of monetary influence. A wealth of human sentiment often lies unseen, untapped, and unappreciated within these experiences. Here, the worth of a heartfelt smile, a cherished memory, or an act of kindness is immeasurable financially.

The first aspect we explore is the immense power of human connection, love, and the simple yet profound act of sharing a moment with someone we care for. A hug shared with a loved one, for instance, brings a warmth that transcends the constraints of financial wealth. The deep sense of satisfaction derived from acts of compassion or kindness, like helping an elderly person across the street, creates a ripple of happiness within us, untouched by monetary transactions. This intrinsic value of human interaction forms a rich vein of joy in our lives, showing us that not all wealth is financial.

Here, we focus on our inherent strengths, such as intelligence, talent, and creativity. Our ability to think critically, solve problems, imagine, and innovate is not dictated by our bank balance. J.K. Rowling, the author of the beloved Harry Potter series, serves as a prime example of this, having dreamt up her wizarding world during a financially challenging period. The fruits of her creativity have since brought joy to millions, and it's worth noting that her immense success was born from her innate talent and imagination, not her financial status.

Further, the self-motivation and determination that drive us towards our goals are also independent of our financial standing. The will to work hard, to strive for better is a characteristic seen across the wealth spectrum. It is a testament to our capacity to find fulfilment in our personal achievements, regardless of the state of our bank account. The joy derived from the process of striving, learning, growing, and ultimately achieving our goals is not priced or sold; it is created and owned solely by us.

Let's consider perception – the ability to appreciate and enjoy the simple things in life. A breath-taking view, the melodic chirping of birds at dawn, the vibrant colours of a sunset, the spellbinding plot of a novel, or the beautiful strokes of a painting – these experiences cost nothing yet offer priceless joy. Our ability to enjoy these aspects of life depends solely on our perspective and not our pocket.

This exploration highlights that while money undoubtedly plays a pivotal role in our lives, it is not the exclusive gateway to happiness. In fact, some of the deepest, most enriching sources of joy are entirely independent of our financial status. As we navigate our paths, it's crucial to recognize, cherish, and harness these sources of happiness beyond the monetary realm. This will give us a more rounded, holistic, and fulfilling perspective of a happy life.

In continuing our exploration into the dimensions of happiness independent of wealth, let us delve deeper into the aspects of life free from the dominion of monetary gain. Recognizing and acknowledging these facets of our existence can further illuminate the nuances of human happiness, enriching our understanding and enhancing our lived experience.

Let's begin by focusing on our health, a vital component of our lives often considered priceless. It's important to understand the distinction between healthcare, which may involve financial investments, and personal health, which is strongly influenced by factors beyond monetary reach. Good health, beyond the aspect of healthcare, encompasses our daily practices and choices – our diet, exercise, stress management, sleep patterns, and overall well-being. These elements that contribute to a vibrant and healthy life are not exclusively purchased but cultivated and maintained through conscious, non-monetary choices.

Then there's the joy of giving and contributing, which far exceeds the value of any currency. Helping a neighbour, volunteering in the community, or lending a sympathetic ear to a friend in need often bestow upon us a deep sense of fulfilment and joy that money cannot buy. The smile of a child you've helped, the relief on a friend's face after a heartfelt conversation, or the appreciation of a community you've supported – these are the rewards that no amount of money can equate to.

Another vital component of non-monetary happiness lies in our self-worth and self-esteem. Recognition and respect from peers or society can often be linked to monetary success, but true self-esteem springs from within. It comes from accepting and valuing oneself, from recognizing one's own accomplishments, and from personal growth. This internal satisfaction and its consequent happiness stand independent of our financial status.

The next pillar we explore is creativity, a space where the human mind flourishes unrestrained by financial constraints. Whether crafting a beautiful piece of art, writing a compelling story, designing an innovative product, or simply finding a novel solution to a problem, creating gives us an unmatched sense of joy and fulfilment. The ability to conceive and execute an idea, to bring something new into the world through one's unique perspective, is not a privilege exclusive to the wealthy.

Furthermore, our relationship with nature offers countless opportunities for non-monetary happiness. The feeling of sand between our toes, the refreshing touch of ocean waves, the serene sight of a forest, or the harmonious sound of a babbling brook – these experiences, rich in joy, come without a price tag. They remind us that our capacity for happiness extends far beyond the realm of fiscal wealth.

Let's consider the bonds of love and care that we form in our lives. The deep connections we forge with our family, friends, and even pets are sources of immense happiness. These relationships, nurtured with love, trust, and mutual respect, bring us comfort, support, and joy that no money can procure.

To sum up, our exploration reveals a profound truth: our happiness is not held hostage by our financial standing. There exists a universe of joyous experiences, fulfilment, and satisfaction that is not bought but lived, felt, and cherished. Acknowledging and embracing these non-monetary sources of happiness can help us lead more balanced, enriched, and fulfilling lives. It's not about negating the importance of money but rather understanding that our pursuit of happiness is a multifaceted journey, with riches found in both the monetary and non-monetary aspects of life.

The energy in the room feels almost palpable as we reach the final phase of this exercise. We have journeyed together through the complex labyrinth of our perceptions surrounding money and happiness. We have unearthed the myriad ways in which we depend on wealth for happiness, and we have also unravelled the many instances where money bears no weight on our joy and contentment. It is a thorough exploration, rich in shared experiences and collective realizations.

As we transition into the concluding step of the exercise, I invite the participants to take a step back and view the results with a fresh perspective. An invitation to look at the two seemingly disparate lists they have helped create – one outlining the areas where money significantly influences happiness and the other highlighting the moments where joy is independent of financial status. I ask them to take a moment and search for any pattern or underlying connection they can discern from these lists.

The room falls silent as participants scan the numerous points jotted down on the flip charts. Their eyes dart back and forth between the two sets of ideas as their minds work to identify any emerging patterns. It's a thoughtful silence, a pregnant pause brimming with potential discovery.

Slowly but surely, a pattern begins to take shape. As participants start sharing their observations, an initial spark of revelation quickly catches fire, illuminating the room with a profound understanding. A couple of brave souls pipe up, pointing out a remarkable pattern that others quickly nod in agreement with – they see that the elements we listed in the second step, those sources of happiness independent of money, all seem to emerge from within the individual. These include moments of personal fulfilment, love, care, talent, creativity, health, intelligence, and perception – intrinsic attributes that are not bought or sold but rather nurtured and expressed.

Contrastingly, the elements listed in the first step, those aspects of happiness that do require money, all appear to be influenced by the external environment surrounding the individual. From education, healthcare, luxuries, status, and security to capital investment and visibility, these factors are linked to the societal structure we exist within and the material commodities we consume.

This breakthrough moment is an inflexion point in the exercise, a critical juncture where participants start to see that the sources of happiness are not monolithic, rather they exist on a spectrum that spans from the individual to the environment. They start to understand that their capacity for happiness does not solely depend on the money they earn or the material wealth they amass. It also comes from the depth of their experiences, relationships, creativity, resilience, health, and capacity to perceive beauty and meaning in the world around them.

This revelation is an eye-opener for many, an illuminating insight that shifts the narrative around wealth and happiness, laying the groundwork for the profound conclusion that is to follow. It brings into focus the notion of agency – of how the individual and the environment interact in determining our sense of happiness. It sets the stage for the overarching theme of the exercise – the role of individual agency in an age of burgeoning AI capabilities.

As the pattern becomes clearer and the participants lean into this newfound understanding, we are ready to delve deeper into the implications of this discovery to understand its significance in shaping our perspective on money, happiness, and the Age of Agency. It's time to bring this newfound awareness into sharp focus and uncover the true power of human resourcefulness.

This pattern of internal versus external sources of happiness isn't just a breakthrough for our exercise participants – it's a rebellious idea that runs counter to many of the messages we receive every day. Society, particularly through marketing and advertising, heavily emphasizes the external sources of happiness. Advertisements lure us with promises of instant joy through material possessions or luxurious experiences, subconsciously reinforcing that happiness lies in our bank accounts. The influence of this pervasive messaging is profound, with most people unknowingly subscribing to the idea that their happiness depends on external circumstances.

The narrative that society purveys often implies that if we don't possess the wealth to access these externalities, we are lacking. The world spins a story in which we need "more" to be happy – more money, possessions, and status. It implicitly ties our self-worth to our financial worth, making us feel deficient if we cannot afford these socially endorsed tokens of happiness. This approach tends to overshadow our internal reservoirs of joy, making us feel inadequate and pushing us towards a never-ending chase for external validation.

This societal messaging becomes all the more dangerous when we examine receiving something for free. At first glance, getting something without a monetary exchange seems like a win. However, when we dig deeper, we discover that this practice can often damage the very sequence of exchange that forms the bedrock of a healthy society and individual self-worth.

When we receive something without offering anything in return, it breaks the value creation and exchange cycle. This can often lead to feelings of guilt, dependency, or inferiority, as the individual may start to believe that they cannot create anything valuable enough to exchange. It indirectly communicates that the person is incapable of producing something worthwhile.

Let's consider an example. Over the years, many developed nations have provided substantial financial aid to African countries. While the intentions are usually noble, the simple act of giving money without expecting something in return can inadvertently send a disempowering message. It implies that the recipients cannot create anything of value in return. This notion is incorrect and perpetuates a dependency cycle and erodes the recipients' sense of self-efficacy.

Of course, this does not suggest that we should stop giving aid or helping those in need. It's merely an invitation to rethink how we can empower individuals and societies, fostering a culture of mutual exchange and recognition of value rather than perpetuating dependency.

Now, imagine a different scenario. Imagine someone creates a product, writes a book, or crafts a poem, and you pay them for their work. This transaction is not merely a financial exchange; it's a recognition of the value they've created. It reinforces their sense of self-worth, and their belief in their ability to produce something of value. It fosters a sense of achievement and fosters happiness that springs from their inner resources, independent of external validation.

In a nutshell, the danger lies not in giving or receiving per se but in ignoring the powerful dynamics of value creation and exchange. We need to emphasize the importance of recognizing and nurturing our internal sources of happiness and understand that while money is necessary, it's not the only determinant of our joy.

In the final part of this exercise, we will delve deeper into the implications of this understanding in the context of the Age of Agency and AI. We'll explore how acknowledging our agency and leveraging it effectively can transform our approach to happiness and wealth creation in this rapidly evolving world.

The grand revelation from the exercise unveils a fundamental dichotomy in our lives. Money isn't the first cause of our happiness; it's our inner power, our personal agency, that creates value and happiness. However, money is necessary to facilitate the exchange of the value we create with the world. In essence, we are the producers of value and creators of our own happiness. This understanding becomes even more crucial as we step into the new era – the Age of Agency – spearheaded by AI.

To make this more tangible, let's consider a clear example. Suppose you have a talent for writing, a passion that comes from deep within. You are not rich in monetary terms, but you possess a wealth of ideas and creativity. In the Age of Agency, this personal talent and passion, combined with AI technology, could birth a successful blog, an online magazine, or even a bestselling book.

Here's how it could work: you leverage AI tools that aid with editing, researching, content generation, and even predicting the content your potential audience would most engage with. Your personal agency – your creativity and talent – remains the foundation's driving force. AI is merely the tool that enhances your creative process and helps you connect with a larger audience. You are not just a writer but an entrepreneur in the Age of Agency.

The content you create, which comes from within you and is augmented by AI, is valuable. It entertains, educates, or inspires people. In return for the value you provide, you receive money through ad revenues, subscriptions, or book sales. Here, money is not the source of happiness but a secondary result, acknowledging the value you have created and provided to others.

This sequence is important. You begin with your own agency to create something valuable. Then, and only then, does money come into play as a facilitator of value exchange. This ensures that your self-worth and happiness aren't tied to money and your innate capacity to create value.

In this new Age of Agency, understanding this sequence and the primary role of our agency is paramount. If we fall into the trap of seeking external validation or chasing after money, we risk becoming passive consumers in the face of advancing AI. However, if we understand that our agency – our creativity, intelligence, talents – is our most valuable asset, then AI becomes an empowering tool, a means to enhance our creative output and extend our reach.

Instead of viewing AI as a job competitor or a threat to our sense of self-worth, we can see it as a catalyst that amplifies our ability to create and deliver value. Whether you're a writer, an artist, a programmer, an entrepreneur, or a teacher, AI can augment your skills, extend your reach, and help you make a greater impact. And in return for the value you provide, you receive money, not as a measure of your self-worth, but as a tool to facilitate further exchanges and to allow for the continuous cycle of value creation and distribution.

This exercise and the subsequent revelations prepare us to navigate the Age of Agency with a new perspective. We are not at the mercy of external circumstances or the whims of AI. Instead, we are powerful agents capable of harnessing AI to amplify our agency, enhance our capacity to create value, and ultimately shape our happiness. By recognizing the sequence – agency first, money second – we hold the key to thriving in this exciting new era.

We close this exploration of personal agency with an inspiring quote that speaks volumes about the potential and power of commitment and decisiveness:

> *Until one is committed, there is hesitancy, the chance to draw back, always ineffectiveness. Concerning all acts of initiative (and creation), there is one elementary truth, the ignorance of which kills countless ideas and splendid plans: that the moment one definitely commits oneself, then Providence moves too. All sorts of things occur to help one that would never otherwise have occurred. A whole stream of events issues from the decision, raising in one's favour all manner of unforeseen incidents and meetings and material assistance, which no man could have dreamt would have come his way. I have learned a deep respect for one of Goethe's couplets: Whatever you can do, or dream you can, begin it. Boldness has genius, power, and magic in it!*

–William Hutchison Murray
(in *The Scottish Himalayan Expedition*, 1951, p. 6)

This quote, steeped in wisdom, speaks to us as individuals and a collective in the business world. It underscores the undeniable fact that every tangible thing in our world, from the mundane to the astonishingly complex – yes, including AI – was once an idea, a decision in the mind of a human.

We live in a world that is largely the outcome of human decisions, shaped by human thought and imagination. Even the advent of AI, significantly altering the business landscape, is a testament to the power of human agency. It was not self-conceived; it was birthed in the minds of humans, nurtured by their decisions, and brought to life by their actions.

Our world is a testament to the power of human agency. As we face the future, armed with new knowledge, insights, and tools, let's remember our role as active agents. The systems, technologies, and ideas we interact with daily are not independent entities but extensions of our own capacity, created and shaped by human agency.

As we navigate the Age of Agency, we must remember the power and magic within each decision we make, each action we take. Our decisions shape our personal trajectories and determine the course of our businesses and societies. The integration of AI into our lives should not eclipse the brilliance of our own agency. AI is a tool, an extension of our capacity, not a replacement for our decisiveness and commitment.

As we step into the future, let us embrace the power of personal agency, commit to our dreams, and chart a path where human decision and AI harmoniously coexist. It is not merely about surviving in the Age of Agency but about thriving, about acknowledging our power and using it to mould our world. As Murray eloquently advises, "Whatever you can do, or dream you can, begin it. Boldness has genius, power, and magic in it." In this Age of Agency, let us dare to be bold.

The Myth of Computer Agency

In 2023, the AI domain once again emphasized the essential role of human involvement and the inherent limitations of AI systems. The tremendous advances made in large language models (LLMs) promised to revolutionize various industries. OpenAI's ChatGPT was central to this wave of enthusiasm, illustrating how generative AI might redefine tasks across diverse business sectors.

However, despite the optimism surrounding this technology, it has some distance to cover before it can reliably assume significant business responsibilities. A prime example of this was the predicament that attorney Steven A. Schwartz found himself in. As reported by Thor Olavsrud in June 2023 on CIO.com, Schwartz, affiliated with Levidow, Levidow & Oberman, turned to ChatGPT for researching legal precedents for a lawsuit against Colombian airline Avianca. To Schwartz's dismay, he soon realized that several cases cited from the AI's output were fictitious, complete with non-existent names, docket numbers, and spurious internal references. The lawsuit, filed on behalf of Avianca employee Roberto Mata for injuries in 2019, became controversial when US District Judge P. Kevin Castel highlighted these discrepancies. Schwartz later expressed regret and committed never to utilize generative AI without rigorously authenticating its outputs.

This mishap reaffirmed the message that while AI's capabilities are ever expanding, human oversight remains indispensable.

Another example that resonates with the limitations of AI was the case of Zillow's home-flipping venture, Zillow Offers, as covered in the same article on CIO.com. Launched in April 2018, Zillow Offers relied on a machine learning (ML) algorithm called "Zestimate" to gauge home values, aiming to purchase, refurbish, and swiftly resell homes. By September 2021, Zillow had acquired 27,000 homes but managed to sell only 17,000. The accuracy issues with the algorithm, which had a median error rate of 1.9% and even escalated to 6.9% for off-market homes, compounded with unpredictable challenges like the COVID-19 pandemic and a labour shortage in home renovations. Consequently, Zillow found itself unintentionally purchasing properties at elevated costs. This miscalculation led to a staggering inventory write down of $304 million in Q3 2021, forcing the company to rethink the viability of the Zillow Offers model.

These incidents emphasize a clear lesson: AI's capabilities are not foolproof. Overestimating AI systems and underappreciating human discretion can have grave consequences. AI should be viewed as an augmentative tool, complementing human intelligence and judgement. The future should revolve around collaborative models where humans employ AI to derive optimal outcomes, always under the careful gaze of human vigilance.

The notion of "computer agency" suggests that AI systems possess an inherent capability to make autonomous decisions. Yet, genuine agency remains a facet unique to humans. Computers, even cutting-edge AI models, operate within predefined confines, processing data and recognizing patterns. Despite their vast processing capabilities, they are void of true independent thought or the dynamism of human decision-making. This is evident from the issues faced by Schwartz using ChatGPT and the challenges Zillow encountered with its Zestimate algorithm. They reiterate that, while powerful, AI systems aren't autonomous entities and don't possess agency akin to humans.

The term "computer agency" can thus be misleading. It suggests an autonomous ability that computers simply do not possess. While AI systems can mimic certain aspects of human decision-making, they cannot fundamentally understand context in the way humans do, to apply ethical judgements, or to make decisions based on nuanced understanding or intuition.

AI systems don't question, they don't doubt, and they don't make decisions in the way humans do. Even the concept of indecision is entirely foreign to AI systems. They operate based on data and algorithms, not on intuition or gut feelings.

It's essential to remember that AI is a tool, not an agent. AI systems are designed to assist humans, augment our capabilities, and automate certain tasks, but they are not designed to replace human judgement or decision-making. The belief that we can fully delegate decision-making authority to AI is misguided and potentially dangerous.

Instead of striving for computer agency, we should aim to cultivate a high-agency culture amongst our people, where humans remain actively engaged in shaping AI's development and application. We must embrace the responsibility to guide AI, set boundaries for its operation, and intervene when necessary. This approach requires understanding that while AI can process data and make recommendations, the final decision should always remain in human hands.

Ultimately, the concept of computer agency is a misnomer. It is a seductive idea, but it does not exist in the literal sense. The belief in computer agency overlooks the inherent complexities of decision-making and the nuances only a human mind can navigate. As we continue advancing in our AI journey, let's remember that the reins of agency should remain in human hands. By doing so, we can leverage AI's capabilities responsibly and effectively and continue to harness its potential while acknowledging and respecting its limitations.

In the dynamic landscape of AI, there exists an intriguing paradox. The fascination with computer agency – the apparent ability of AI systems to act autonomously and make independent decisions – has been a captivating narrative in our techno-centric society. We marvel at the progress of AI, its ability to perform complex tasks, sift through vast amounts of data, and make predictions with precision. Yet, as we see in many real-life examples, the concept of computer agency is, in reality, a mirage. It is an apparency, not a fact.

Now, consider the flip side of this coin, the less-explored and often underappreciated aspect – human agency. Herein lies the great irony. We have a remarkable power that exists in actuality – human agency – the capacity of individuals or teams to act independently and make their own free choices. Yet, we often overlook this, entranced by the phantom of computer agency.

Let's consider this: we've all seen or known someone who excels in their role, be it Jimmy from the local McDonald's or Jane from the neighbourhood library. They're not just performing their tasks efficiently; they're adapting to changes, making decisions on the fly, and bringing a personal touch to their roles. These individuals aren't just executing instructions; they're employing human agency. They're making choices, taking the initiative, and owning their actions. This is an aspect of intelligence that is profoundly human and currently beyond the capabilities of any AI.

Why, then, is there not as much marvel at human proficiency? Why do we not invest as much time and energy in cultivating and harnessing this human agency as we do in chasing the elusive concept of computer agency?

The AI systems we develop and admire are, after all, products of human agency. They are borne out of our choices, creativity, and capacity to solve problems and innovate. Even the most advanced AI is still fundamentally a tool created and guided by human agency. It does not possess agency itself; it is an extension of ours. Every breakthrough in AI, every triumph, is a testament to human ingenuity and decision-making.

Despite the allure of AI autonomy, the reality is that AI is limited. It cannot make genuine choices. It operates within the boundaries defined by its programming and algorithms, lacking the capacity for indecision or true decision-making. It cannot understand or replicate the complexity of human thought and the depth of our emotional spectrum. Even the most advanced AI cannot compare to the richness of human intelligence and the dynamism of human agency.

While we continue to develop AI and strive for advancements, let's not lose sight of the incredible capacity we already possess – human agency. Let's invest in nurturing this human ability. Let's appreciate the proficiency of Jimmy, Jane, and millions of others who exhibit human agency every day. Let's not just celebrate AI achievements; let's also celebrate the human capacity that makes these achievements possible.

In doing so, we may find that the key to unlocking the full potential of AI doesn't lie in the mirage of computer agency but in the reality of human agency. Let's embrace this irony and leverage it, not just for advancing AI, but for enriching human society. The human–AI future we envision isn't one where AI supersedes humans but one where AI enhances human agency, empowering us all to achieve more.

Chapter 3

The Power of Observation, Resourcefulness, and Creativity

The Vital Importance of Observation

In this chapter, we will delve into an interactive exercise that I first encountered during my time at Microsoft. Two internal consultants there used this approach during a root-cause workshop, and its efficacy was immediately apparent to me. This compelling exercise, centring on the Washington Monument, unfolds a crucial facet of problem-solving and highlights our habitual inclinations when addressing challenges. It offers a hypothetical yet captivating scenario surrounding the monument's disintegration.

Since that introduction at Microsoft, I've incorporated this method as a cornerstone opener for my workshops worldwide. As I sought to cite the original author of this technique, I encountered many versions across countless web pages, each interpreting the core concepts in its unique way. However, the trail eventually pointed to Don Messersmith, a professor emeritus at the University of Maryland. His study on the lighting of the memorials in Washington D.C. has evolved into a foundational reference for this root-cause methodology. The

DOI: 10.4324/9781032684895-4

scarcity of his original document has led to the proliferation of varying "creative" versions of the tale, including my own.

Here's the fictional problem statement: the Washington Monument is disintegrating.

Let me guide you through this interactive exercise just as we would in a workshop, aiming to reproduce its vibrant and engaging atmosphere in this written format. While we can't converse directly as we would in a workshop, I'll do my best to make it feel like we are in a face-to-face conversation. While I will be responding to this exercise, I urge you to engage fully with each question – ponder and generate your answer before reading on. This personal touch will deepen your learning experience.

Let's dive into our Washington Monument example together.

We're starting with this problem statement: the monument is disintegrating. "Where would you start if this were your real-life challenge to solve?" Give it some thought.

"Have you got it?" I'm going to suggest that we start with a basic question, no matter how obvious it may seem.

Question 1: Why is the monument disintegrating?
>   The answer we have is that harsh chemicals are being used to clean it. Now that we've unearthed this fact, how might you solve this problem?
>   Take a moment if you need to. Despite what we might assume about why a monument needs cleaning, it's essential to validate our assumptions. Hence, I propose another question.

Question 2: Why are harsh chemicals being used?
>   The answer is that we need to clean the pigeon poop.
>   Now, how would you solve this problem? With an inquisitive mindset, we wouldn't take for granted why the pigeons are there. The vast skies and the slender monument prompt another question.

Question 3: Why are there so many pigeons?
>   Our answer to this is that they eat spiders, and there are a lot of spiders at the monument. Now, how would you solve this problem? If you've identified that we need to probe further instead of making assumptions, you're spot on.

Question 4: Why so many spiders?
>   You may have an idea about this one. The answer is they eat gnats, and there are lots of gnats at the monument. No assumptions here, only enquiry. I'm sure you see the pattern by now.

Finally, we arrive at question 5: Why so many gnats?
>   And the answer, surprisingly, is they are attracted to the light at dusk.

This leads us to a pivotal moment where the strings of all our questions and answers tie together to reveal an elegant and simple solution: turn on the monument's lights later to avoid attracting gnats.

By actively engaging with each question, we've unravelled a chain of cause-and-effect leading back to a seemingly unrelated issue: the timing of when the monument's lights are turned on. This is a powerful testament to the effectiveness of this approach. The hands-on, deeply thoughtful participation sets a robust foundation for our further journey into the world of AI.

At a glance, the exercise might appear to have a straightforward solution. However, the objective here isn't simply to discover a solution but to discern the nature of the solution's "elegance," to understand how we as human beings approach problem-solving, and what hampers us from finding root causes and elegant solutions.

As revealed through this exercise, an elegant solution can be measured against the dual criteria of time and money. For instance, a seemingly valid solution like "changing the cleaning chemicals used" might appear harmless, but what does that entail? Conducting numerous lab tests, sampling concrete from the monument, and spending time, resources, and money to find a chemical that won't harm the monument. In comparison, adjusting the lighting schedule requires minimal time and resources but effectively addresses the root cause.

Throughout this exercise, several insights surface. One, we often default to more obvious and often more complicated solutions. Take the example of the proposed solution to "kill the pigeons." This one-sentence solution, albeit in jest, unveils the complexities that could arise if implemented, highlighting the need to think beyond immediate fixes.

Two, we often fall into the assumption trap, basing our solutions on past experiences rather than present observations.

Lastly, our innate desire to help often rushes us towards solutions without fully understanding the problem. This haste is reinforced by a cultural bias that rewards quick answers and discounts questions, a habit formed early on in our schooling.

The key takeaway is to foster a culture where enquiry reigns supreme, where questions are revered, and issues are dissected to their very core. This is the essence of observation: a deep-rooted desire to discern the true nature of things. Such an approach invariably leads to the most efficient solution, optimizing both time and cost. The relevance of this approach spans beyond corporate boardrooms, permeating city governance, our homes, and our individual lives.

This revamped approach to problem-solving can be adopted in different aspects of our lives. It's not just about solving complex business problems or addressing civic issues but also about dealing with daily hurdles in our personal lives. Let's begin with the boardroom, an apt microcosm of problem-solving in action.

In many organizational cultures, there's a rush to provide answers. Employees, especially in front of their bosses or peers, feel an urge to quickly propose a solution rather than appearing ignorant or indecisive. This propensity to jump to conclusions not only hampers the quality of solutions but also inhibits a culture of learning and curiosity.

As leaders and decision-makers, we need to foster an environment that values questions more than quick answers. It is not ignorance but a desire to deeply explore and understand the problem. Encourage teams to investigate thoroughly, ask why repeatedly, and challenge their assumptions. This creates a culture of curiosity and learning, where problem-solving becomes a journey of exploration and discovery.

We need to start rewarding curiosity; the willingness to probe deeper. It should be celebrated when someone raises a hand to ask a question. A culture that appreciates enquiry not only stimulates creative problem-solving but also encourages continuous learning.

In a rapidly evolving world, learning agility – the ability to learn, unlearn, and relearn – is a crucial competency. By valuing questions, we enable individuals to remain lifelong learners, adaptable to changes, and proactive problem-solvers.

But this transformation shouldn't be confined to the boardroom. Our schools, homes, and public spaces can all benefit from a culture that values understanding over knowing. It's crucial that our young learners are not just rewarded for knowing the answers but also for asking insightful questions.

At home, foster a sense of curiosity and a habit of questioning among children. Encourage them to ask "why" and appreciate their inquisitiveness. This will cultivate a mindset that sees problems not as hurdles but as opportunities for learning and exploration.

In our cities and communities, we can apply the same principle. Engage citizens in civic problem-solving by encouraging them to probe deeper into issues rather than accepting surface-level explanations. This leads to more informed, involved citizens and more effective, sustainable solutions to communal problems.

Let's take a moment to reflect on the power of the human mind, the importance of enquiry, and the unique capabilities that we, as humans, possess.

This exercise in root-cause analysis and deep questioning serves a dual purpose: first, it underscores the importance of adopting an attitude of enquiry when tackling problems – whether they be complex business challenges or the concepts presented in this book. Approaching problems with curiosity and an open mind, rather than a "know-it-all" attitude, is crucial. It's not just about finding quick solutions, it's about understanding the problem in its entirety, asking the right questions, and being open to new ideas and perspectives.

This attitude of enquiry isn't only applicable to the workplace or academia – it is also relevant to your journey as a reader of this book. As we delve into different concepts, theories, and examples, you're encouraged to approach each chapter with curiosity and openness. There will be new propositions, complex arguments, and paradigm-shifting ideas. To truly reap the benefits of this book, you need to examine these ideas critically, ask questions, and strive for a deeper understanding. An attitude of "knowing best" can hinder this process of discovery and learning.

Second, this exercise showcases the remarkable ability of the human mind to assimilate disparate concepts and data points. Our capacity for observation, our ability to make connections, and our knack for understanding context are all uniquely human capabilities. They are what separate us from machines and AI.

While AI can execute tasks, analyse data, and learn from experiences, it lacks the human ability to fully comprehend the intricacies of a problem. AI doesn't understand context in the way humans do; it cannot assess the emotional responses of others or grasp the subtle nuances that often come into play in real-world situations. This is where human agency truly shines – we can understand problems deeply, find elegant solutions, and guide the use and development of AI technologies for maximum benefit.

So, as we move forward, I urge you to harness the power of human agency. Embrace the attitude of enquiry. Challenge assumptions. Delve deeper into problems. Understand that your ability to comprehend, see the larger picture, and empathize is unmatched by any machine. And remember, the greatest discoveries often come not from knowing the answers but from asking the right questions.

This journey we're embarking on is not just about exploring the capabilities of AI – it's about understanding the unique strengths of human intelligence, the power of enquiry, and the joy of discovery. Let's explore this fascinating interplay of human agency and AI together.

We just explored the importance of diving deep into the problem's core instead of treating symptoms or immediate issues. But how do we ensure we are not falling into the traps of assumption and hastiness in problem-solving? How do we ensure the elegance of our solutions?

The short answer is by questioning and actively engaging with the problem. However, doing so in real-world situations requires overcoming a few ingrained biases and habits. Let's delve deeper into these obstacles and explore ways to circumvent them.

We usually employ our prior experience as a reference when encountering new problems. This ability to draw from past experiences is valuable, but it can also lead to assumptions that may cloud our ability to see a problem clearly in the present context.

In the Washington Monument exercise, it would have been easy to assume that the monument was deteriorating due to natural causes or harsh weather conditions, given the common knowledge about the wear and tear of buildings over time. This assumption could have led us to costly, labour-intensive solutions such as using special protective coatings or moving towards an expensive restoration process.

In reality, the root cause was the timing of the lights, a solution far simpler and cheaper to implement than any of the assumed ones. Here lies the danger of assumptions. They lure us into false paths, away from the true root cause, and in turn, away from an elegant solution.

The key lies in fostering a culture of inquisitiveness. The tendency to ask questions, even when we believe we know the answers, allows us to challenge our assumptions. When we ask, "Why are harsh chemicals being used?" instead of assuming it is due to standard cleaning practices, we open the door to understanding the problem at a deeper level.

This might sound simple, but it goes against the grain of most of our educational and professional training. We're often rewarded for quick solutions and penalized for seeming ignorance. Therefore, posing questions, especially when we're expected to have answers, can feel counterintuitive. However, the strength of our solutions lies in the quality of our questions.

It's not to say that experience has no value. Indeed, it does. It helps us narrow down the field of search. It gives us a direction, but it should not provide the destination. The destination must be found by exploring the present situation, asking questions based on what we see now, and engaging with the problem at hand.

As we question and actively engage with the problem, the path to an elegant solution begins to form. Elegance here doesn't refer to a sophisticated or intricate solution, quite the opposite. An elegant solution is most efficient in terms of time and resources and directly addresses the root cause of the problem.

The elegance of turning the lights on at a later time in the Washington Monument example lies in its simplicity and directness. It was not a solution that sought to combat the consequences; instead, it aimed to eliminate the problem from its source.

Achieving such elegance in our solutions requires an active restraint from jumping to conclusions and a willingness to invest time in understanding the problem's nuances. It calls for patience and a shift in our approach towards problem-solving.

This chapter implores us to embrace questioning, challenge our assumptions, and strive for elegance in our solutions. As we equip ourselves with these tools, we move closer to our goal of effectively handling problems in various domains of our lives.

We also prepare ourselves for the coming discourse on AI. As we navigate the intricacies of AI, these problem-solving skills will play a critical role in ensuring that we address the right problems and find elegant solutions. We'll delve deeper into this in the following section. For now, reflect on your problem-solving approach and the place of assumptions, questions, and elegance.

One cannot overstate the depth and richness that human observation brings to problem-solving. The faculties through which we engage with the world – listening, perceiving, noticing, reading, analysing – are an ensemble that creates a symphony of insight that AI cannot replicate. This is an intrinsic advantage that we have as humans; our senses and cognition allow us to discern nuances and context beyond AI's capabilities.

For instance, a human observing a conversation can perceive subtle shifts in tone, recognize the unspoken through body language, and understand the cultural and emotional contexts that pervade the dialogue. We weave together our understanding, empathy, and instincts to better understand human interactions. This perception level makes humans natural problem-solvers in complex situations. On the other hand, AI can analyse vast amounts of text or data with remarkable speed, but it lacks the depth of understanding and the richness of human experience.

Moreover, our ability to observe is not limited to just using our senses. We can reflect, introspect, and draw from the reservoir of our ideas and emotions. We can also be innovative in our observations, looking at situations through different lenses, combining perspectives, or noticing patterns hidden in plain sight. This fusion of empathy, creativity, and critical thinking defines human observation as an art form in itself.

It is essential to understand that AI and human observation are complementary. While AI excels in enduring tasks and processing large volumes of information, human observation adds qualitative depth, emotional resonance, and context that AI cannot perceive. By synthesizing the endurance of AI with the finesse of human observation, we can form an incredibly potent combination for problem-solving.

As we move forward in an increasingly AI-driven world, let's not lose sight of our unique strengths. Our observation is not just a sensorial experience but a blend of cognition, emotion, and creativity. The realization and appreciation of this capability are indispensable in asserting our unique value in an ecosystem where AI continues to grow in prominence.

The Unmatched Power of Human Resourcefulness

Resourcefulness isn't merely an innate human ability – it forms the cornerstone of our agency. Agency, the capacity to act independently and make free choices, enables us to exert control over our lives and surroundings. This agency is catalysed by our capacity for resourcefulness, equipping us with the tools and techniques necessary to effectively navigate our path, especially when faced with challenges.

The dynamics of resourcefulness are as diverse as our society itself. It doesn't differentiate between socio-economic statuses or geographical boundaries. The bustling hallways of Fortune 500 companies witness it, as do remote, resource-scarce villages. From the lone entrepreneur ingeniously navigating market uncertainties to create a thriving business out of a mere idea to the rural teacher transforming a one-room schoolhouse into a vibrant learning environment with limited resources, the range and depth of human resourcefulness are illuminated in these disparate scenarios.

Resourcefulness is the quiet, relentless engine behind every business success story, driving innovation, fostering adaptability, and propelling growth. It's the golden egg coveted across industries. It enables us to create the remarkable from the mundane, whether it's a physical structure, a community, or a thriving business. This is creativity in its purest form, an authentic human phenomenon fundamental to the business world, education, healthcare, and numerous other sectors.

However, we find ourselves in an age of paradoxical fear, where concerns about job displacement and the devaluation of human skills have accompanied the rise of AI. Here lies the irony: while AI has demonstrated remarkable capabilities in performing structured tasks and analysing large datasets, it operates within a framework, unable to deviate much from these parameters or innovate in the face of the unexpected. Despite its sophistication, AI does not attempt to emulate human resourcefulness – it thrives in predictable situations, whereas resourcefulness emerges from uncertainty, ambiguity, and unpredictability.

Given this stark contrast, the fear of AI replacing human roles seems unfounded, even absurd. When juxtaposed with the dynamism of human agency, AI's lack of resourcefulness underlines the misplaced concerns about AI undermining our roles. The very trait driving innovation and change in our world, resourcefulness, is beyond AI's grasp. The importance of human agency, fuelled by resourcefulness, cannot be overstated in the Age of AI.

Recognizing this isn't enough. We must champion this invaluable trait and commit to nurturing it. This means fostering an environment that encourages creative thinking, problem-solving, and adaptability. Our educational institutions, workplaces, and societal structures need transformation to cultivate this invaluable human trait actively. As we move deeper into the AI age, it's our resourcefulness that will provide us with a competitive edge, enabling us to flourish amidst technological advancements.

As we journey further into the era of AI, celebrating and enhancing our unique human capacity for resourcefulness become more critical than ever. This trait will enable us to exercise our agency, harness the potential of AI, drive innovation, and navigate the uncertainties of the future. The value of human resourcefulness, a key catalyst for our agency, will not just endure in the Age of AI – it will flourish.

This is best conveyed via examples.

The Bootstrap Entrepreneur

Jeff lives in a quaint town, far removed from the bustling start-up scene of metropolitan areas. While the city skyline is populated with dreams of grandeur and tech enterprises, Jeff's aspirations are no less significant. He envisions a tech venture – an app that would serve as a bridge between local farmers and consumers. It's a direct-to-door service, eliminating middlemen, and ensuring that the produce on your table is as fresh as it gets. But with dreams so big, the path is inevitably riddled with challenges, especially given Jeff's limited resources.

With not enough funds to rent an office space or hire a professional team, Jeff's drive and resourcefulness become his greatest assets. His first priority is crafting a prototype for his app. Without the capital to hire a professional developer, Jeff leverages generative AI. This innovative tool helps him produce code and assemble an early prototype without incurring significant costs.

However, a major breakthrough came when he entered into a joint venture with a progressive farmer from the area. Recognizing the potential in Jeff's idea, the farmer offered resources such as office space, basic infrastructure, and most importantly, a direct insight into the everyday challenges farmers face. In exchange, the farmer would receive early access to the app's marketplace. This partnership was invaluable. It provided Jeff with early customer validation opportunities and ensured that the app he was building was rooted in the real-world needs of the farmers.

Equipped with a rudimentary version of his app, Jeff then approached the town's largest restaurant. By emphasizing the direct farm-to-fork model, he convinced the restaurant owner to give the app a try. This allowed the establishment to select the freshest produce, at unbeatable prices, directly from the source. Engaging with a real customer even before the app's final iteration, Jeff could iron out practical issues that might have been overlooked in a traditional development process. In essence, his financial constraints forced him into a position that offered invaluable real-world testing, a benefit that abundant resources might have denied him.

For the promotional phase, Jeff couldn't tap into high-end advertising channels. Instead, he used social media. By sharing the story of his app and engaging with potential users, he not only marketed his product but also used these platforms for invaluable market research. Online surveys, feedback from early users, and live Q&A sessions turned into crucial data points for refining the app.

Financing, however, was a steep mountain to climb. Traditional investors, wary of an entrepreneur without a track record and based in a small town, remained hesitant. But Jeff was undeterred. Leveraging the joint venture with the farmer and the deal with the restaurant, he created a compelling crowdfunding campaign. The narrative, focusing on sustainability and the tangible benefits for both farmers and consumers, resonated deeply. Funds poured in, enabling Jeff to take the next crucial steps.

As he transitioned into the operational phase, Jeff's resourcefulness continued to shine. Rather than hire a full-time team, he sought out remote freelancers, focusing on their skills irrespective of their location. This strategy minimized costs while tapping into a talent pool that might have been overlooked by traditional businesses.

In retrospect, Jeff's journey exemplified the power of resilience and resourcefulness. Faced with obstacles at every turn, he transformed each challenge into an opportunity, proving that with determination and innovation, even the most ambitious dreams can be realized.

The Resourceful Teacher

In a picturesque village embraced by mountains, Maria shoulders a unique responsibility. This remote village, untouched by the rapid developments of city life, is home to a singular one-room schoolhouse where Maria plays the vital role of the sole educator. She's tasked with the daunting challenge of teaching a diverse group of children, each at different academic levels. However, rather than viewing these as hurdles, Maria's indomitable spirit transforms them into platforms for inventive teaching methodologies.

The school's shortage of textbooks could have easily stunted the learning process. However, Maria, ever the resourceful teacher, initiated a book-collection drive in neighbouring towns. She liaised with local communities, businesses, and philanthropic organizations. But books were just the beginning. Embracing the digital age, Maria managed to acquire second-hand computers for the school from a charitable institution. With the digital world at their fingertips, her students were ushered into a vast realm of online educational resources.

Harnessing the potential of technology, Maria introduced her students to AI. Realizing the capabilities of generative AI, she granted her senior students access to it. This AI not only promptly answered their queries but also empowered them to design micro lesson plans. Under Maria's guidance, these older students then mentored the younger ones. This novel approach not only enhanced the educational experience for the younger children but also instilled a deep sense of responsibility and pride among the senior students.

The younger students weren't left out from the wonders of technology. Whenever Maria introduced a new concept, she ensured it was paired with a visual – be it a picture or a video. This brought the outside world into their classroom, providing them with contexts and examples they might never encounter in their mountain village.

The power of collaborative learning was further magnified when Maria introduced parents into the educational mix. On designated days, parents, rich in their local expertise, would volunteer at the school. They shared their skills, from weaving to traditional storytelling. And for subjects outside their domain, generative AI came to the rescue. With its aid, even parents became students first, learning new concepts, and then transitioning into teachers, passing on their newfound knowledge. This inclusion of parents not only enriched the curriculum but also fostered a stronger bond between generations.

Maria also emphasized hands-on learning. Utilizing locally available resources, lessons took a tangible form. Stones, sand, and leaves became tools for geographical lessons. Everyday items, from fruits to utensils, demystified complex mathematical concepts. Complementing this, Maria also championed holistic development. The children, through initiatives like tree planting and village clean-ups, were instilled with values of environmental conservation and civic responsibility.

Maria's journey exemplifies the transformative power of resourcefulness paired with technology. By seamlessly integrating generative AI into her teaching approach, she not only overcame logistical challenges but also crafted a rich, holistic, and dynamic learning environment. Her story transcends mere academic achievements, weaving together lessons in community, curiosity, and responsibility.

The Adaptable Farmer

In a quaint agricultural town, Samuel, a tenacious farmer, grapples with the complexities of erratic weather and the escalating expenses of farming essentials. Despite his crops producing diminishing yields, placing his family on the precipice of economic challenges, Samuel refuses to be overwhelmed. Instead, he taps into his deep well of resourcefulness, setting in motion a revolutionary transformation of his agricultural methodologies.

Confronted by the whims of unpredictable weather, Samuel recognizes that conventional farming techniques fall short in these evolving circumstances. He realizes he must stay ahead of the curve. Investing in a basic weather station, Samuel delves deep into understanding local weather nuances. Yet, his most game-changing move is incorporating AI into his weather interpretation system. By doing so, he achieves astoundingly accurate predictions regarding rainfall patterns and other meteorological factors, which drastically reduce the risks associated with farming and simultaneously optimize his harvest.

Faced with the soaring prices of modern farming equipment and chemical supplements, Samuel's innovative spirit emerges once more. Unable to procure the latest machinery or pricey fertilizers, he immerses himself in the world of sustainable farming. He crafts organic fertilizers using farm by-products, such as crop remains, manure, and compost. Additionally, he integrates natural pest deterrents, such as beneficial insects and specific plants. These organic solutions not only reduce costs but also elevate the vitality and yield of his crops.

The constraints in irrigation are met with yet another of Samuel's ingenious solutions. Implementing a homemade drip irrigation system crafted from locally sourced materials, Samuel ensures optimal water usage, providing his plants with just the right amount of moisture directly at the roots.

Recognizing the broader shift in consumer behaviour, Samuel aligns himself with a burgeoning local movement championing sustainable and conscious eating. These individuals, committed to pesticide-free, ethically produced food, often find difficulty sourcing produce that meets their strict criteria. Seeing this gap, Samuel adapts his farming practices and guarantees that his farm's produce adheres to their rigorous standards. This pledge creates a surge in demand for his crops among local retailers and restaurants. His farm's certification becomes a sought-after seal of approval, a symbol of purity and ethical farming.

Furthermore, to diversify his revenue streams, Samuel earmarks a section of his farm for beekeeping. The honey harvested becomes an alternate source of income, and the bees, in their natural routine, pollinate his crops, thereby augmenting the yield.

Samuel's journey is a testament to the power of innovation and adaptability. By fusing technology with traditional farming, aligning with sustainable movements, and making judicious decisions, Samuel not only safeguards his farming venture but elevates it to new heights of productivity and prosperity.

The Resilient Community Leader

In the heart of an economically challenged neighbourhood, we encounter Jane, an indomitable community leader burning with a drive to better the lives of her fellow residents. Facing issues like funding shortages, dilapidated infrastructure, and societal hurdles, Jane's spirit remains unyielding. Through her relentless pursuit of betterment, she demonstrates that even amidst adversity, the spark of human ingenuity can ignite transformation.

Jane's surroundings are marred by decaying infrastructure, with government resources often funnelled elsewhere. Recognizing the dangers of relying on external aid, Jane formulates an idea to harness the latent potential within her community. Her attention is drawn to a long-neglected lot, forgotten and decrepit, that she believes can become the beating heart of revitalization.

Driven by her vision, Jane sets out to convert this abandoned land into a fertile community garden. With a tight budget but bursting with zeal, she understands the need to mobilize her community's spirit. Using generative AI, Jane orchestrates a robust marketing campaign, crafting a compelling website, engaging social media posts, and vibrant flyers. This sophisticated technology, combined with her genuine enthusiasm, galvanizes the community. Her door-to-door campaigning gradually turns initial scepticism into collective excitement.

With the community now rallied behind her, Jane's next task is to rejuvenate the forsaken lot. Rather than lamenting the absence of landscaping professionals or top-tier garden supplies, she leans into her community's strengths. A neighbourhood-wide clean-up day is initiated. Old tyres metamorphose into quirky planters, and discarded bricks are given a second life as garden trails. The message is clear: treasures can be unearthed in the most overlooked places.

But a garden is nothing without its flora. Jane reaches out to local garden enthusiasts, nurseries, and homeowners, persuading them to donate plants and seeds. The response is heartening, and soon the barren land is awash with green.

Among the lot's forgotten structures is an old shed, which Jane, in her typical fashion, visualizes as an opportunity. She revamps it into a state-of-the-art hydroponics centre – the first in the community. Using online resources, she nurtures a group of "hydroponics ambassadors," empowering them with knowledge which they, in turn, share with others. The remarkable progress is showcased on social media, attracting eco-conscious individuals from neighbouring areas, eager to contribute their insights.

Witnessing the buzz generated by Jane's initiatives, the town's administration sits up and takes notice. Seeing an opportunity to align with this grassroots movement, they pour in resources for infrastructural development and even become hydroponics ambassadors, further cementing the initiative's credibility.

To maintain and expand the operations, Jane cleverly monetizes the hydroponics centre. By charging a modest fee for its organic produce, she ensures the community has access to nutritious, sustainably grown food, while generating enough revenue to keep the project thriving.

Jane's tale is a testament to human resilience. Through the harmonious marriage of technology and sheer willpower, she showcases that the spirit of innovation, especially when fortified with the wonders of AI, can reshape communities and lives. Her journey embodies the strength of human resourcefulness, proving that with dedication and ingenuity, one can chart a path to progress, regardless of the challenges at hand.

Through the stories of Jeff, the innovative entrepreneur, Maria, the resourceful teacher, Samuel, the adaptable farmer, and Jane, the resilient community leader, we've seen first hand how resourcefulness can transform challenges into opportunities, breed resilience, foster innovation, and spur growth. Their narratives offer a vivid testament to the boundless potential and dynamism of human resourcefulness.

Each of them faced unique obstacles that could have impeded their progress. Yet, they defied these odds by exercising their innate resourcefulness, demonstrating that constraints can often be the birthplace of creativity. Jeff improvised his technological solution to an emergent problem, Maria used unconventional tools to offer her students a quality education, Samuel adjusted his farming practices to combat climate change, and Jane transformed a neglected lot into a vibrant community garden.

Their stories show that resourcefulness isn't just about finding a way to meet our needs; it's about pushing boundaries, challenging norms, and striving for better despite adversity. It's about seeing the potential where others see limitations, being creative in the face of scarcity, and having the courage to act upon our ideas to bring about change.

In a world increasingly reliant on AI and automation, these narratives underscore the irreplaceable value of human resourcefulness. While AI is proficient at executing tasks within predefined boundaries, it cannot think beyond those boundaries and innovate in ways that humans can. It cannot navigate the grey areas and uncertainties that our world is riddled with, areas where human resourcefulness thrives and truly shines.

Therefore, now more than ever, it is essential to reaffirm the significance of nurturing this vital human trait. As we stand on the threshold of a new era, an era of AI and other technological advances, our focus must be on fostering environments that encourage and reward resourcefulness. We need to reconfigure our educational systems, workplaces, and societal structures to promote this invaluable attribute actively.

Resourcefulness, this silent, relentless engine of human progress, will continue to drive innovation, foster adaptability, and propel growth in this new age. The stories we've explored illuminate this truth, reinforcing that the value of human resourcefulness will not just endure in the Age of AI – it will flourish.

As we journey deeper into the era of AI, let's ensure that we continue to champion and enhance our unique capacity for resourcefulness. After all, it is this trait that will enable us to harness the potential of AI effectively, drive innovation, and navigate future uncertainties. Our resourcefulness will be our compass, guiding us through the uncharted territories of this brave new world. It is a testament to our unparalleled human agency, a beacon of hope in the face of adversity, and a reaffirmation of the unmatched power of human resourcefulness.

Creativity in an AI-Dominated World

In a world increasingly steeped in AI, the essence of what makes us uniquely human becomes a precious commodity. One key facet of this is our innate creativity, a "magic" that machines have yet to replicate. It is this ability to think laterally, to connect ideas, and to dream up innovative solutions to problems that truly sets us apart.

Every single man-made object in our world – and indeed beyond it – began its journey as a spark of thought within the human mind. These thoughts evolved, growing from rough ideas to comprehensive plans, from plans to models, and ultimately into tangible reality. This is the process of creation, a uniquely human endeavour that carries with it a profound responsibility. It is our birthright and our duty to create, a power that no computer can ever wrest from us. In fact, the birth of ideas, the germination of innovation, relies entirely on human ingenuity.

This human creativity, the ability to invent and reimagine, is at the heart of artistic expression, scientific discovery, and societal progress. Despite the leaps and bounds made in AI, AI remains incapable of such original thought. Its existence and progress remain wholly dependent on our input and capacity to birth ideas.

In an era defined by AI, the value of human creativity has never been more apparent. While AI excels in optimization and refining processes based on existing data and patterns, the human capacity for creative thought truly disrupts the status quo, leading to revolutionary innovations. Our ability to imagine new possibilities, think abstractly, and take calculated risks, is something that AI simply cannot mimic.

Human creativity is vital in the professional world, fuelling strategic planning, problem-solving, and innovative advancement. While AI may shoulder the burden of data analysis and repetitive tasks, human creativity ignites novel ideas, strategies, and solutions that can ultimately transform a business. From the initial spark of inspiration to the culmination of a successful project, human creativity is the driving force.

Recognizing the importance of creativity in this AI age, it becomes crucial that we foster this innate ability. This includes promoting a culture that values creative thinking, embraces diverse perspectives, encourages curiosity and exploration, and provides opportunities for creative expression and risk-taking. Both in education and in the workplace, environments that stimulate, rather than stifle, creativity are essential.

As we traverse this increasingly AI-dominated landscape, understanding and nurturing our "magic" – this human spark of creativity – becomes paramount. This uniquely human trait sets us apart from machines and equips us with a crucial advantage in the face of rapid technological advancement. We must embrace and cultivate this creative potential to thrive in our AI-driven future.

The concepts of observation, resourcefulness, and creativity are often intermingled in discussions of human ingenuity. While these facets of human potential certainly overlap, it is beneficial to delineate the unique characteristics of each.

Observation is the cornerstone of human understanding, allowing us to perceive and interpret the world around us. It is the process by which we gather information through our senses, recording the details and nuances of our environment. An accomplished artist, for instance, does not merely see a landscape; they observe the way light and shadow play across the land, the subtle shifts in colour and texture. This level of observation then influences their interpretation and rendition of the scene.

Conversely, resourcefulness involves making the best use of available resources to solve problems or overcome obstacles. It demands a certain level of adaptability, of thinking on one's feet. Picture a stranded traveller with a flat tyre in a remote location without a spare. Instead of succumbing to despair, they might use their resourcefulness to fashion a temporary fix – perhaps creating a tyre repair kit from the material they have on hand.

Lastly, creativity encompasses the ability to generate original and innovative ideas, pushing boundaries and challenging the status quo. The spark turns an observation into a novel concept and harnesses resourcefulness to manifest it into reality. For example, a chef who experiments with unconventional ingredients and techniques to create a unique dish is exhibiting creativity.

While these concepts are distinct, they also interact in powerful ways. Observations can trigger creative ideas; creativity often requires resourcefulness to realize these ideas; resourcefulness is enhanced by keen observation of available resources. These three qualities – observation, resourcefulness, and creativity – are interdependent gears in the engine of human innovation.

To harness the full potential of these attributes, we must foster an environment that encourages keen observation, nurtures resourcefulness, and stimulates creativity. This is the key to surviving and thriving in a world increasingly dominated by AI. By nurturing these uniquely human qualities, we ensure that the "magic" of human ingenuity continues to shine brightly, driving us forward in an ever-evolving world.

Chapter 4

Harnessing Human Agency in an AI Era

Autonomy, Passion, and Personal Growth

Let's begin this chapter by setting a foundational premise: anything autonomously produced by AI now establishes the benchmark for "average." However, this new "average" is remarkably high. Those who have previously coasted on being merely "average" may find themselves at a disadvantage and could understandably feel threatened by AI. But we, as humans, have the capacity to surpass this benchmark. Equipped with our inherent powers of observation, resourcefulness, and creativity, we have the potential to employ AI to elevate beyond anything AI can generate.

Our new imperative is to consistently eclipse this evolving standard of average. It's about infusing our unique human touch, imprinting our work with a stamp of human brilliance. Let AI serve as a measure, a yardstick, that we should strive to outpace. In essence, we leverage AI as a foundation, amplifying its outputs with our own innovative flair. We harness AI's capabilities, then extend them with our distinct human ingenuity.

We are well into a paradigm shift in our understanding of work and the nature of employment itself. For countless generations, most people have viewed work as a necessary evil, a means to an end, a way to put food on the table and pay the bills. The prospect of finding joy and fulfilment in our work was a luxury few could afford. This mentality has tethered millions of workers worldwide to jobs that drain them physically and mentally, with scant personal fulfilment.

DOI: 10.4324/9781032684895-5   **41**

In previous years, there might have been a kernel of truth to the belief that work was simply a means to survive. But today, in the AI era, this notion is becoming increasingly antiquated. As technology evolves, our perspective on work and the opportunities it presents also evolves.

The current and emerging technological landscape empowers individuals to align their passions with their professions. The proliferation of digital tools and the growing accessibility of technology have made it easier than ever for anyone to turn their passion into a lucrative career. This transformation means that the age-old axiom of doing what you love doesn't have to be a pipe dream anymore. More importantly, it doesn't mean that pursuing what you love equates to compromising on financial stability or success.

More specifically, a work model has gained momentum that aligns closely with personal passions and flexibility: the gig economy. This modern labour market, fuelled by the rise of digital technologies and the internet, is characterized by the prevalence of short-term contracts or freelance work as opposed to permanent jobs. Various digital platforms have made it easier for individuals to find gig work that matches their skills and passions. Instead of adhering to traditional employment contracts, people now trade their services on demand, enjoying the freedom to choose when, where, and how they work.

Digital technologies and the internet largely facilitated the development of the gig economy. AI has since played a significant role in enhancing and scaling the gig economy, but it wasn't the initial catalyst for its emergence.

Moving closer to home, consider your present job. Regardless of what it is, you can earn well doing what you genuinely love. There are two critical aspects when considering your work environment: Do you have a deep-seated passion for what you do? And do you have the ability to earn a good living from this passion?

Whether you're a corporate employee, a freelancer, or an entrepreneur, the objective is to align your passion with your profession, creating a synergy where you can enjoy your work while also earning a sustainable income.

To underscore our message, consider the example of John. He's not just a jeweller but a man of varied passions: he loves reading, writing, creating jewellery, and travelling. By applying the principles and framework from this book, John has crafted a business model that seamlessly integrates his distinct passions and skills.

John used this framework to make sound business decisions, identifying his "superpower," and selecting a flagship product he was passionate about: handcrafted jewellery. He leveraged technology to boost his productivity and took an innovative approach to his go-to-market strategy. He found a way to integrate his love for travel into his business model, deepening his connection with local cultures and deriving immense personal satisfaction from his work.

Just as John the Jeweller found autonomy and financial success through technology, many people in the gig economy find the same advantages. AI has played a critical role in this transformation, facilitating the matching of gig workers with potential job opportunities, optimizing work processes, and even handling administrative tasks such as invoicing and payment processing. Moreover, AI-powered platforms offer personalized job recommendations, aiding individuals to find gigs that align with their skill sets, passions, and preferred work styles.

It's important to understand that the format of how you work isn't as crucial as the passion you derive from your work. In John's case, he leveraged technology to create a unique, globally influenced jewellery business that brings him joy and financial success.

In this book, we'll explore this concept further, providing insights on how to integrate your passion into your work, leverage technology to enhance your productivity and reimagine your own go-to-market strategies. The future of work is here, and it's filled with opportunities for both personal fulfilment and financial success.

In the traditional work paradigm, an individual's level of autonomy was largely contingent on their position within a hierarchical structure. However, with the emergence of digital tools and AI technologies, the scope for personal autonomy in the workplace has expanded exponentially. It is now increasingly possible for individuals to carve out their own niche, set their own working parameters, and still achieve financial success.

The rising gig economy and the advent of AI have enabled individuals to not just witness a shift in the nature of work but also participate in shaping this new landscape. The ability to pursue work they love, coupled with the flexibility offered by the gig model, enables individuals to address their unique personal and professional demands more effectively. The narratives of many gig workers mirror John's journey, integrating work with personal growth, autonomy, and fulfilment. AI acts as a powerful enabler, ensuring seamless interactions in this new marketplace and promoting the efficient exchange of services.

This radical shift towards personal autonomy has significant implications for job satisfaction and work–life balance. It means you no longer have to be tied to a rigid 9–5 work schedule; you can decide where you want to work from, and most importantly, you can decide what you want to work on. The expanding landscape of remote work, fuelled by technological advancements, provides unprecedented opportunities for individuals to redefine their work experiences.

Let's return to our example: John the Jeweller. He exemplifies this new era of autonomous work, where he can decide his work processes, from creation to sales. This autonomy allows him to pursue his passions for jewellery-making and travel simultaneously, opening a world of experiences and inspirations directly feeding into his work.

Moreover, his use of technology optimizes his jewellery production and enables an innovative sales strategy. By leveraging digital systems, he can minimize his risk, maximize his agility, and evade traditional costs associated with a physical retail presence. He holds no inventory and compensates his primary supplier based on sales, keeping his costs low, and risk minimal.

The marriage of autonomy and technology in John's work method reflects a key aspect of the future of work. Technological advancements are continually providing opportunities for individuals to optimize their work processes, bring innovative products and services to market, and reach global audiences, all the while maintaining a level of autonomy that was unthinkable just a few years ago.

Importantly, this shift is not just for entrepreneurs. Freelancers and corporate employees alike can leverage technology to redefine their roles, optimize their contributions, and potentially transform their industries. Whether utilizing data analytics for informed decision-making, leveraging AI for process automation, or using digital platforms for reaching new audiences, integrating technology can significantly elevate the scope and impact of your work.

While autonomy and technology open the door for redefining work experiences, a more profound shift is on the horizon – a shift towards work that provides financial stability and promotes personal growth and transformation.

Work is no longer just a means to a pay cheque. Instead, in the AI era, it can be a platform for self-discovery, personal development, and self-expression. When your work aligns with your passion and leverages your unique skills, it can be deeply fulfilling and lead to unparalleled growth and evolution.

Reflecting on John the Jeweller's experience, we see how his entrepreneurial path is intertwined with personal growth and exploration. His travels inspire his jewellery designs and foster a deep connection with various cultures worldwide. His love for travel is not just a leisure activity but a fundamental aspect of his work that fuels his creativity and connects him more deeply to his passion.

His story is not without its challenges. However, these challenges are growth opportunities, prompting him to be creative, innovative, and adaptable. As he navigates his business, he learns new skills, embraces new technologies, and adapts to new environments. This constant learning and adaptation are integral to his personal growth.

Further, his blog, where he shares his cultural encounters and jewellery pictures, is more than a promotional platform for his products. It's a creative outlet that lets him express his experiences, ideas, and learnings. The thought of getting published someday not only fuels his ambition but also elevates his quest from a job to a deeply fulfilling vocation.

This personal transformation, facilitated by embracing autonomy, leveraging technology, and aligning work with passion, represents the future of work in the AI era. This paradigm shift transforms work from a necessary chore into a path of self-discovery and personal growth. Whether you're an entrepreneur, freelancer, or corporate employee, this new era offers you the chance to rethink what work means to you and unlock your potential.

The AI era heralds a new dawn for the world of work, one where autonomy, technological advancement, and personal growth are not just aspirational concepts but tangible realities. It's an era where doing what you love and earning well from it doesn't have to be a pipedream. With the right mindset, strategies, and tools, you can redefine your work experience and pave the way for a fulfilling and successful career.

As we delve deeper into the AI era, a transformative shift is evident, touching not only the realms of entrepreneurs and freelancers but also traditional businesses. The advent of remote work serves as a mere glimpse into these changes, hinting at deeper structural transformations beneath the surface.

In many of today's well-managed corporates, the conventional employer–employee relationship is being revolutionized. Companies are increasingly resembling marketplaces or platforms, facilitating the exchange of specialized services between internal stakeholders. Imagine an accountant offering his expertise to the HR manager, not as a dictated task from a hierarchical structure, but as a value proposition, much like a freelancer would pitch to a potential client.

Instead of being bound by rigid job descriptions, employees are evolving into service providers within their own organizations. Gone are the days when employees were solely evaluated by hours at their desks; now, they're assessed by the quality and efficacy of the services they provide. Essentially, in this reimagined corporate marketplace, employees serve their internal "customers," channelling the mindset and agility of freelancers.

In this evolving landscape, the line between the employer and the "employee" is blurring, and a new model is emerging that embraces the principles of autonomy, passion, and personal growth. This shift means that regardless of where we sit on the spectrum – entrepreneur, freelancer, or corporate employee – we all have an exciting opportunity to reshape our work lives in this new era. We can apply this fresh perspective to enhance our individual work experiences, contribute to our fields more effectively, and direct our personal steps towards fulfilment and success.

Our Glaring Achilles Heel

Technology often takes the limelight in the celebration of progress, frequently stealing the show with its dazzling choreography of efficiency and precision. AI, the prima donna of this spectacle, is often revered for its capabilities. But beneath the shimmering veneer of awe and reverence, dissecting the fundamental forces at play is crucial, for they illuminate a telling story about our collective human attributes.

Reflecting on our fascination with AI, it is vital to underscore a fundamental truth – the vast spectrum of human capability far outstrips the prowess of any AI without contest. The multifaceted brilliance of the human mind shines across various realms – judgement, decision-making, interpretation, understanding, communication, and discerning preferences, to name just a few.

Imagine, for a moment, the richest, most complex piece of art you've ever encountered. Each brush stroke tells a tale, each colour sings an emotion, and each texture invokes a sensory response. This intricacy and nuance mirror the depth and complexity of human faculties, capabilities that AI, in its most advanced form, can only crudely mimic.

If AI were to be personified, it would resemble an individual hampered by significant constraints. It would be like a person with severe cognitive limitations and sensory deficits, devoid of emotions, incapable of creative thought or spontaneous decision-making, and incapable of understanding and communicating complex concepts effectively. Yet, despite these glaring limitations, our fascination with this level of "intelligence" borders on the obsessive. But why?

The conundrum lies not in the superiority of AI but in its contrasting attributes – consistency and predictability – traits that we, humans, often struggle to maintain due to our mercurial natures and susceptibility to distractions. It's a bizarre paradox – our superior capabilities get eclipsed by our fallibility in maintaining discipline. In this light, the allure of AI seems less about its capabilities and more about it compensating for our behavioural shortcomings.

In the spotlight of our exploration is this notion of discipline, an intrinsically human trait, yet ironically, its scarcity has bolstered our reliance on machines. This narrative isn't about pitting human against machine. Rather, it is about deciphering why, despite its apparent inferiority, AI remains a focal point of admiration.

Discipline and its counterpart, distraction, are two sides of the same coin in human behaviour. The aptitude to concentrate, maintain diligence, and pursue consistent efforts despite obstacles differentiates disciplined individuals. In contrast, susceptibility to distractions, whether in the form of the latest binge-worthy series, rampant social media scrolling, or more insidious forms like substance abuse, fractures our focus and hinders productivity.

Ironically, as we celebrate our creative leaps, innovations, and ability to strategize and emote – traits that remain unmatched by any AI – our Achilles heel seems to be our struggle with maintaining discipline. The inconsistencies in our behaviour, borne out of our lack of discipline, present a challenge to the predictable, efficient mechanics of business operations.

This takes us to the heart of why AI often outshines human capability in business operations, despite its limitations. AI's principal charm lies in its unwavering consistency, its ability to remain unfazed by the myriad distractions that beleaguer the human mind. The allure is not merely about AI's capacity to methodically plough through voluminous datasets, a task we might find monotonous or overwhelming. Instead, it is about its ability to function in a disciplined, predictable manner, day in and day out.

We've grown to appreciate and rely on AI because it provides us with a measure of certainty. Machines don't succumb to distractions or moods; they don't have bad days or bouts of unproductivity. They offer a steady rhythm of work that businesses enjoy, a rhythm that is often disrupted by the human propensity towards unpredictability.

However, this isn't a tale of despair for humanity or a push for machine supremacy. Instead, it explores our nuanced relationship with technology and calls for introspection about our work ethics. It's about realizing that while AI can compensate for our shortcomings in some areas, we, as humans, bring unrivalled value in creativity, emotional intelligence, and strategic thinking to the table.

The collective fascination with AI isn't about seeking compensation for human shortcomings. Instead, it shines a spotlight on a vital pattern: the appreciation of machine-like discipline. This appreciation isn't limited to machines; it is generously extended to humans who exhibit similar levels of self-discipline. We revere athletes, entrepreneurs, artists, and others who demonstrate exceptional discipline in their respective fields. It's an appreciation born out of reliability; a machine, just like a disciplined human, is unlikely to let us down. This shared admiration reveals a fundamental aspect of our value system – a steadfast commitment and discipline, whether in silicon or flesh, is highly respected and desired.

Imagine the potential transformation if we apply a dash more discipline to our already vastly superior human faculties. If an entity as inherently limited as AI can command such admiration due to its unwavering discipline, imagine the admiration a more disciplined human could garner.

This isn't an invitation to espouse robotic rigidity. It's a call to action, a prompt to utilize our agency to make better choices for ourselves and those around us. This could involve small yet significant changes: eating better, engaging in regular exercise, ensuring adequate sleep, and curbing excessive drinking, among others. The objective is to enhance our reliability by nurturing the discipline required to keep our word once given.

The viral social media message, "Choose your hard," encapsulates this ethos perfectly:

Marriage is hard. Divorce is hard. Choose your hard.
Obesity is hard. Being fit is hard. Choose your hard.
Being in debt is hard. Being financially disciplined is hard. Choose your
hard.
Communication is hard. Not communicating is hard. Choose your
hard.
Life will never be easy. It will always be hard. But we can choose our
hard.
—Pick wisely.

– Unknown

This poignant message delineates the inevitability of hardship in all life choices and prompts us to exercise discernment in our decisions. The underpinning message is one of self-improvement and the exercise of discipline.

The hype around AI serves as a wake-up call. We, as humans, need to raise the bar. We can't afford to languish in self-imposed restraints, undermining our profound abilities with a lack of discipline. AI's growing influence should not be perceived as a threat but as a catalyst driving us towards personal betterment.

The impetus to improve our discipline is clear. Failing to do so risks rendering us redundant, our creativity overshadowed by inconsistency and unpredictability. As businesses grapple with the trade-off between our superior abilities and our lack of discipline, the appeal of AI's steadfastness grows stronger. Even the minutest decrease in the gap between human and AI capability magnifies this risk. We need to act, not out of fear but from a place of empowered agency, to ensure that the future of work remains irrevocably human.

Crafting a Growth Manifesto

In this age of burgeoning AI technology, as we traverse uncharted territories where human frailties and strengths are being increasingly spotlighted, we face a crucial need to firmly establish our values. The risks of leaving this to happenstance are far too great, and we're not talking about a superficial list of values, handled solely by the Human Resources department. What's demanded is a clear, impactful manifesto whose singular objective is to fuel organizational growth.

At the heart of this proposition is intentionally addressing human contribution within organizations. As AI permeates every facet of business, voids will inevitably emerge if we fail to recognize and define the specific role of human ingenuity and creativity in shaping our future. Never before has the need for a clearly articulated design principle been so paramount – a beacon guiding the path of human growth so that we remain the masters of AI.

Leaving such pivotal directives to chance is a risk too grave to take. Businesses lacking a clear design principle are gambling with their futures, perhaps unknowingly. We need to consolidate these guidelines within a potent growth manifesto that embraces and addresses the multifaceted nuances outlined in this context.

In the grand scheme of things, the growth manifesto isn't just a directive; it's a lifeline. It maps the dynamic interplay between humans and AI, serving as a tool to navigate the complexities of the AI-driven landscape. It's a call to action for organizations to take the reins of their destiny, strategically defining the human role in their growth trajectory rather than surrendering their fate to the unguided evolution of AI.

Hence, in the era of AI, crafting an intentional, human-centric growth manifesto isn't just a strategic move; it's an existential necessity.

In the spirit of embracing the essence of the Human-Centred Growth Manifesto, we present a representative framework illustrating the operationalization of the manifesto's principles. This is not a fixed guide, but a dynamic blueprint intended to evolve and adapt in tandem with organizational growth and technological advancements. Thus, we call it a "Growth Manifesto Blueprint," encouraging readers to use this as a starting point for their internal culture code.

Value 1: Mutual Understanding

Mutual understanding stands as the cornerstone of our Growth Manifesto Blueprint. It is not just a principle but a commitment to open communication, active listening, and thoughtful consideration of diverse perspectives. It is a conviction that every voice matters and that open, respectful conversation can lead to profound insights and fruitful collaborations. In an Age of AI and automation, this human-centric value takes on an even greater significance.

Why is this so? Let's begin by emphasizing that AI does not "understand" in the way humans do. Regardless of its sophisticated responses, AI computes based on a series of probabilities. Essentially, AI is making educated guesses, and it has become adept at getting them right. Humans inherently seek, perhaps even crave, genuine understanding. This innate human quality and desire fosters real connections. True understanding is what resolves both large and small conflicts, aligning individuals and fostering agreement. It ensures we empathize with another's perspective. While AI can simulate this to an extent, its imitation falls short of genuine human understanding. No matter how convincing AI's semblance of comprehension may be, our innate human desire will continually drive us towards authentic understanding for as long as our hearts beat.

In an era marked by the pervasive influence of AI, the value of mutual understanding takes on a new dimension. It's not merely about fostering harmonious relationships or facilitating effective collaboration. It's about actively resisting the easy temptation to let AI mediate our interactions through generated or suggested responses, reducing them to transactional exchanges stripped of emotional nuance. It's about consciously prioritising human connection and genuine dialogue over the convenience of automated, AI-mediated communication.

AI holds immense potential for enhancing efficiency and decision-making capabilities. However, as we continue to delegate tasks and decisions to these intelligent systems, there's a danger of losing touch with the inherently human element of collaboration and understanding. We risk replacing meaningful, rich dialogues with sterile, algorithmic determinations. We run the danger of forgoing the empathy, the emotion, and the authenticity that underpin the human experience for the expediency of machine logic.

This is why mutual understanding is critical. It reminds us of the importance of seeing through another's lens, of striving to comprehend their truth, however challenging it might be. It encourages us to bypass the AI intermediary when necessary and address issues directly, as individuals, teammates, and humans. This ability to preserve our human-centric approach in an increasingly AI-dominated landscape is, in essence, the reason mutual understanding is fundamental to fostering growth.

Through understanding comes empathy; through empathy, collaboration; and through collaboration, innovation. And in the Age of AI, this cycle has never been more crucial. It's a cycle that places mutual understanding at its core, as a beacon guiding us towards sustainable, meaningful growth, even in the face of rapid technological advancement. This is why mutual understanding is a key value in our Growth Manifesto Blueprint – it's not just a principle but an active stance, a way of being that shapes our approach to growth in the era of AI.

Consider a medium-sized tech start-up, for example. There are several teams. Each focused on different aspects of the company's product. However, there seems to be a disconnect between the design and development teams. The design team's creative, user-focused approach doesn't quite mesh with the developers' more pragmatic, feasibility-oriented approach. The result? Frequent miscommunications, delayed projects, and a product that could be more seamlessly integrated.

Incorporating the principle of mutual understanding, the company's leadership implements regular cross-team meetings. Here, each team is encouraged to update the others on their progress and share their perspectives, challenges, and thought processes. The goal is not to reach an immediate consensus but to foster an understanding of each other's viewpoints, roles, and limitations.

Over time, the regular discussions lead to a shift in the company's culture. The designers start to understand the constraints and considerations of the developers. The developers, in turn, appreciate the user-centred thinking that drives the designers. This understanding breeds a more collaborative environment. It's no longer a matter of pushing responsibility or finding fault but about finding solutions together. This mutual understanding, born from active communication and respect, fuels innovative problem-solving and efficient workflows. As a result, the company's growth accelerates, and its product improves significantly.

This simple scenario demonstrates the immense power of mutual understanding in driving growth. It's about more than just avoiding conflict or fostering a positive work environment. Mutual understanding promotes a deep, empathetic engagement with differing perspectives, a fertile ground for innovation, efficiency, and growth.

In the Age of AI, where technological capabilities constantly evolve, the need for this deeply human principle becomes more acute. AI may automate tasks and processes, but the human element – our ability to understand, empathize, and collaborate – will be the real driver of sustainable growth. This is why mutual understanding is a key value in our Growth Manifesto Blueprint, not just as a principle but as a commitment, a way of operation, and ultimately, a way of being.

Value 2: Play to Win

In a world increasingly shaped by digital transformation and AI innovation, the second value we propose in our Growth Manifesto Blueprint is to "Play to Win." This value, rooted in a spirit of playful competition and passionate commitment, serves as a guiding principle for how we navigate the often-tumultuous landscape of growth.

To "Play to Win" is to approach our endeavours with a blend of intensity and joy, fuelled by an unwavering commitment to our goals. It is not about playing recklessly or obsessively, focusing exclusively on winning at any cost. Instead, it's about engaging enthusiastically and fully in the task at hand, always keeping in mind the ever-evolving rules of the digital game. Our approach reflects a mindful balance: we play with vigour, but we also enjoy the game.

When we "Play to Win," we also pay attention to the integrity of the game. It's not merely about the final score or the immediate outcome; it's about how we achieve those results. The value we place on the journey – the learning, the challenges, the resilience, the teamwork – is as significant as the destination itself. We measure our success not just by the victories we attain but also by how we play the game.

In an era dominated by AI, this value becomes even more critical. AI systems and digital technologies have revolutionized how we play the game of growth, from automating routine tasks to providing analytics for decision-making. While these tools can enhance efficiency and provide valuable insights, they can also unintentionally encourage a single-minded focus on results, neglecting the human elements of teamwork, creativity, and ethical conduct.

The value of "Play to Win" reminds us that, as we navigate the AI-infused landscape, we must maintain our human-centric approach. It's about harnessing the capabilities of AI but never losing sight of our human values and the spirit of playful competition. It encourages us to leverage AI as a tool for achieving our goals but also to remember that the passion, creativity, and integrity we bring to the game truly define our success.

Imagine a tech start-up developing an AI-based solution. The team is diverse, with engineers, data scientists, UX designers, and more. Everyone is passionate and committed to the project. They work long hours, fuelled by the vision of their innovative product. But amidst the intense work, they maintain a spirit of playful competition. They have brainstorming sessions where wild ideas are encouraged, celebrate small wins along the way and value each other's perspectives. They play hard, but they also enjoy the game. Even when challenges arise, they tackle them together with the same vigour and positivity. This is the essence of "Play to Win."

The value of "Play to Win" in our Growth Manifesto Blueprint represents an approach to growth that is both intense and enjoyable, serious yet playful, and results-driven but also values-oriented. It's about acknowledging the power of AI and digital tools in transforming the game while cherishing the human spirit that makes the game worth playing.

Value 3: Earned Success

Value three in our Growth Manifesto Blueprint, "Earned Success," encapsulates our conviction that true success isn't simply given or stumbled upon. Instead, it is the fruit of work, dedication, and skill. It's the genuine accomplishment that comes from producing tangible products, creating meaningful outcomes, and making measurable impacts.

"Earned Success" stems from a belief that the worth of our work should be judged based on what we produce – the actual results of our efforts. These results are the result of our actions, such as completed projects, developed products, or achieved goals, are a testament to our skills, creativity, and dedication. They reflect the value we've brought into the world through our work.

In contrast, performance metrics – the rewards we receive in exchange for our efforts, like monetary gain, recognition, or support – are often the more commonly recognized symbols of success. These metrics are a consequence of the work we put out into the world. Obviously enough, money comes in as an exchange after the product is made. Worrying about money alone distracts us from our real work of getting good products into the world.

In our AI-infused world, where algorithms often measure success in terms of arbitrary performance metrics, our commitment to "Earned Success" is a call to refocus on all elements of value creation. It emphasizes that while AI and digital technologies can aid in measuring outputs and even in optimizing processes, they should not dictate what success means. At the end of the day, it's not just about a single arbitrary metric but more about the quality and impact of what we produce.

Let's consider an illustrative example. A writer, let's call her Ana, spends months painstakingly crafting a novel. She pours her creativity, time, and effort into creating a compelling narrative and complex characters. After countless late nights and revisions, she finally finishes her book. Before we get to the sales numbers, her performance metric, Ana has already achieved an aspect of "Earned Success" by creating a quality product. She has created something of value that didn't exist before. It's a testament to her dedication, skill, and effort.

Moreover, suppose Ana's novel ends up resonating with many readers, influencing their perspectives or offering them solace in difficult times. Her sales skyrocket as a result. In that case, the market response to her work adds another layer to her "Earned Success" – a measurable indicator that extends beyond the immediate product she crafted.

To elaborate on the example of Ana, let's imagine that she decided to utilize ChatGPT, an advanced AI, to assist in creating portions of her novel. With this tool at her disposal, her role would evolve. She would give the AI an outline of her plot and guide the character development, enabling the AI to generate high-quality text. As a result, Ana could focus more on the aspects of the writing process she enjoys most and excels at – creating compelling narratives and complex characters.

Yet, Ana's contribution would not just be limited to these areas. By carefully guiding and tweaking the output of ChatGPT, she would be infusing her unique insights and creativity into AI-generated content. Her value-add or work done, then, wouldn't be any less; instead, it would be redefined, transformed in line with the evolving digital age.

However, to ensure her work is valuable, Ana's novel has to be appreciated and enjoyed by others. The performance metrics, the sales and acclaim her book receives, become crucial in this context. Without reader engagement and validation, her book might remain an unnoticed masterpiece. So while her own work is a testament to her creative process, the performance metrics capture the market's reception of her work.

It's a delicate balance between creating something of personal significance and ensuring it resonates with others. Achieving success, therefore, involves optimizing both work done and the associated exchange this brings.

In an increasingly digitized world where AI has the potential to augment and transform our capabilities, focusing on performance metrics will be increasingly important. It's about ensuring that our work not only creates value but that it also reaches and is appreciated by the right audience.

In forthcoming parts of this book, we will delve deeper into this topic, discussing some practical tools. These tools can greatly assist in optimizing performance metrics, which is critical in a digitally dominated landscape. The aim is to ensure that the value we create holds significance for us and reaches, resonates with, and is appreciated by the intended audience. The Age of Agency heralds an era where the focus on these performance metrics, the evidence of our earned success, becomes increasingly paramount. Stay tuned as we navigate these fascinating shifts together.

Value 4: Customer-Centric Service

The fourth value, "Customer-Centric Service," speaks volumes about our commitment to others, especially our customers. This value reinforces the idea that service is not a transaction but a relationship that hinges on empathy, professionalism, and deep listening. It calls for a paradigm shift in our approach, treating service as an opportunity to connect, understand, and create value.

In this context, professionalism is not just about adhering to rules or standards. It's about embodying respect, responsibility, and ethical conduct. In a world where interactions with AI systems are increasingly common, this human touch of professionalism differentiates us, adding a sense of reliability and trustworthiness that AI cannot emulate.

Consider Ben, a customer-support representative. When faced with a frustrated customer, he does not resort to a standard script or a quick fix like an AI support system might. Instead, he listens carefully, asks insightful questions, and takes the time to truly understand the problem. He employs his professionalism to provide a comprehensive solution, communicating clearly and respectfully and ensuring the customer understands the steps he's taking. This approach changes the customer's perception positively.

However, in the evolving landscape of AI, the role of professionals is transitioning towards becoming consultants or specialists. Technology continues to offer generic solutions, but the unique human ability to perceive, comprehend, and interpret nuanced data becomes even more critical. In customer service, this means understanding customers' unique circumstances and needs rather than prescribing one-size-fits-all solutions.

Imagine Ben in this light. As a skilled professional, he doesn't just offer support but serves as a consultant, providing personalized solutions. Rather than pushing a standard script or a generic solution, he strives to comprehend the specifics of the customer's issue. He exercises empathy and patience, creating an environment where the customer feels heard and understood. His professionalism prompts him to probe deeper and understand why the problem occurred, what unique factors might have led to it, and how it can be prevented.

This principle of "Customer-Centric Service" extends beyond the traditional definition of customer service. Whether we are product developers considering the needs of end-users or HR managers providing personalized advice to colleagues, the commitment to understanding and serving our customers is crucial. This comprehensive application of "Customer-Centric Service" involves genuine care, professionalism, active listening, and a steadfast commitment to place the customer at the centre of the decision-making process.

The Age of AI brings forth a need for humans to elevate their roles, observe, understand, and connect on a deeper level. This applies in every interaction with every customer, whether internal or external, and across all sectors of an organization. The human touch, combined with the power of AI, can lead to unparalleled customer service and foster sustainable growth that is deeply resonant with people's true needs and desires.

In every transaction or interaction, the act of deeply understanding the problem at hand precedes the search for a solution. Akin to a good doctor who attentively listens to her patient's unique concerns before suggesting any treatment, we, too, need to approach our customers with a similar depth of understanding and intentionality. This involves resisting the tendency to supply generic solutions or simply endorsing solutions suggested by the customer or drawn from our past experiences.

Even in this Age of AI, where we can leverage powerful tools to assist in problem-solving, the quality of the solution is intrinsically tied to the richness of our understanding of the problem. As humans, we become crucial in collecting precise and comprehensive data through observation, enquiry, and empathy. The more specific and thorough our data is, the better equipped we (and the AI tools we employ) are to create a solution that resonates with the customer's unique needs.

This is the core principle of "Customer-Centric Service." In the Age of AI, this ability to listen, understand, and consult in an in-depth and personalized manner gives us a significant edge. This professional approach allows us to deliver profoundly human and deeply personalized value and, ultimately, drives sustainable growth.

In this modern landscape, characterized by rapid advancements in AI and automation, delivering what's expected requires less script and more agency. Let's take a closer look at Ben, our customer-support representative. If Ben's value is anchored solely in his ability to deliver a standard script, his role becomes vulnerable. An AI Chatbot can be programmed to deliver a script, often faster and without human error. In contrast, Ben's unique human skills – his capacity for empathy, creativity, and resourcefulness, for instance – are irreplaceable. This is where agency comes into play.

Agency, in this context, refers to the ability to make independent choices and decisions, listen attentively, think critically, and devise creative solutions. It's about possessing the autonomy and the skills to navigate complex situations, understand nuanced problems, and deliver personalized services. In essence, it's about taking ownership of one's role, being proactive, and going beyond the script to truly serve the customer.

Companies, too, need to make this transition from script to agency. Businesses that continue to rely heavily on scripts, protocols, and one-size-fits-all solutions risk falling behind. Such methods lack the flexibility, personalization, and deep understanding that a human professional exercising their agency can provide. The competitive advantage, therefore, lies in fostering a culture that encourages and rewards agency.

Investing in human agency – in skills like active listening, empathy, critical thinking, and problem-solving – becomes paramount. These skills differentiate us from AI, making our services more personal, more attuned to individual needs, and therefore, more valuable. This human touch, coupled with the efficiency of AI, can deliver customer service of unmatched quality and effectiveness.

The good news is that human agency can be developed and nurtured. By cultivating a work environment that encourages learning, creativity, and autonomy, businesses can empower their employees to take initiative, think out of the box, and deliver solutions that truly resonate with the customer's unique needs. Investing in developing these skills and fostering this agency is an investment in sustainable growth and customer satisfaction.

As we navigate through the Age of Agency, let us remember that our most valuable asset is our ability to understand and connect with others on a human level. Customer-centric service is, at its core, a celebration of this uniquely human capacity. It is a call to action for us to exercise our agency, transcend scripts, and offer services that are as unique, personal, and human as we are.

This pursuit of agency and a steadfast commitment to customer-centric service will set us apart in this AI-dominated landscape. It will enable us to provide services that are not only effective but also deeply meaningful, creating experiences that echo with our customers long after the transaction is complete.

Value 5: Honesty and Integrity

Our fifth value, honesty and integrity, stands as an unwavering pillar of our blueprint. These aren't simply aspirational buzzwords; they are our binding commitments, the principles that guide every decision, every interaction, and every pursuit we undertake. Sustainable growth and success are built on a foundation of trust, and this trust is cultivated through consistent honesty and integrity.

In an AI-dominated landscape, this commitment to honesty and integrity has become more vital than ever. AI systems are only as good as the data they are fed. If an AI is exposed to falsehoods, distortions, or misleading data, it will learn and replicate accordingly, which could lead to disastrous consequences. From giving wrong solutions to making misleading predictions, the ripple effect of dishonesty in AI is far-reaching and potentially detrimental to us as individuals, as professionals, and as a society.

Moreover, AI's ability to test and scrutinize data makes dishonesty risky. An AI performing basic data interrogation could easily expose a seemingly harmless white lie in a meeting. The embarrassment and loss of credibility resulting from such exposure could significantly impact one's professional standing. In the Age of AI, where transparency and traceability are the norms, we must strive towards honesty as a fundamental virtue. We stand to gain, personally and professionally, when the truth is spoken and our actions align with our commitments.

Integrity, too, is spotlighted in this AI-driven era. It is about staying true to your beliefs and being resilient amidst the flurry of narratives and sentiments that circulate, often accelerated by generative AI. If we don't firmly hold onto our beliefs and stand up for the truth, we risk being swayed by the amplified sentiments of a minority who may appear like a majority due to AI replication. Our ability to discern, adjudicate, and observe becomes more crucial than ever before.

The second aspect of integrity is about maintaining our standards. The temptation to accept AI-suggested solutions without critical examination might be strong, especially given the efficiency and convenience offered by these tools. However, an unquestioning acceptance of AI solutions can lead to flawed decisions. It is incumbent upon us to exercise discernment, maintain high professional standards, and resist the allure of a quick fix.

Companies must adapt to this changing landscape by revising their processes, adding validation steps, and mitigating areas of vulnerability where decisions could be made based on a superficial "first glance." Human inspection, analysis, and decision-making must remain integral to the process, reinforcing the necessity for honesty and integrity.

As we move deeper into the Age of AI, our commitment to honesty and integrity must strengthen. As humans, we have an unparalleled capacity for judgement, empathy, and morality – qualities that AI cannot emulate. Let's leverage these qualities, exercising them responsibly and consistently to counterbalance the potential pitfalls of our AI-infused world.

As we continue our quest in this rapidly evolving landscape, let us be more honest, act with greater integrity, and promote transparency in all we do. There has never been a more critical time than now to uphold these virtues. As we do so, we contribute to creating an environment that fosters trust, encourages responsible AI usage, and supports sustainable growth.

Value 6: Observation, Resourcefulness, and Creativity

Our sixth value is the cultivation of observation, resourcefulness, and creativity. This principle fosters a culture that encourages problem-solving, innovation, and adaptability. Here, constraints are seen not as barriers but as challenges to overcome, spurring growth and innovation. Through our creativity and ingenuity, we redefine what's possible, striving to make the impossible possible.

Resourcefulness is a powerful human trait that sets us apart from anything else. It stems from our innate drive to thrive and succeed, even when faced with seemingly insurmountable challenges. This resourcefulness leads us to make something from nothing, transforming an empty canvas into a masterpiece, a blank page into a stirring novel, or a simple idea into a ground-breaking innovation.

Returning to the example of Jeff, a start-up founder who dreams of creating a unique app that bridges the gap between local farmers and urban consumers. He doesn't have the resources to compete with big companies or a large team to delegate tasks to. All he has is his idea and an unwavering belief in its potential. But it's his resourcefulness that propels him forward. He learns how to code using generative AI, understands the ins and outs of app marketing, and reaches out to his network for support. Despite limited resources, he successfully creates the app, eventually seeing it succeed in the marketplace. This is the power of resourcefulness.

With its ability to learn from large amounts of data and execute tasks efficiently, AI is a powerful tool. But it is still a tool devoid of dreams, goals, and the will to succeed. It does not possess the human ability to make something from nothing. It cannot envision a goal and tirelessly work towards it, despite countless hurdles and setbacks. This distinct human quality of resourcefulness, powered by our dreams and aspirations, gives us an edge that AI cannot replicate.

In an AI-dominated world, these qualities are not just desirable; they're essential. The capability of an AI system to learn, process, and even predict is impressive, but it is our uniquely human traits of observation, resourcefulness, and creativity that set us apart and give us the edge.

Take Olivia, a project manager at a tech company. When an unforeseen issue arises in a crucial project, an AI system could present a range of solutions based on the data it has been trained on. But Olivia's keen observational skills help her notice a nuanced aspect of the problem that the AI missed. Her resourcefulness leads her to consider out-of-the-box solutions, and her creativity helps her envision a unique approach that isn't just a reactive solution but a proactive strategy that could prevent similar issues in the future.

Or consider Alex, a digital marketer. When an AI-driven marketing campaign isn't generating the expected results, it doesn't rely solely on data analytics to adjust the strategy. He observes and tries to understand the sentiments and needs of the target audience, something that an AI might not fully grasp. His resourcefulness comes into play when he adapts the campaign to better resonate with the audience, while his creativity shines when he devises a novel concept that distinguishes the brand in the crowded marketplace.

Creativity might seem to be under threat in a world where AI systems can generate art, write articles, and compose music. But it's important to remember that AI can only generate what it's been trained to create. It cannot observe the world, absorb its wonders, and reflect them in its creations as a human can. It doesn't have the resourcefulness to adapt and improvise when faced with an unforeseen situation. This is where our human creativity truly shines.

In a business context, this means a company that encourages observation, resourcefulness, and creativity in its workforce is more likely to stay ahead in the Age of AI. Such a company could leverage the strengths of AI to optimize processes and improve efficiency while tapping into the uniquely human potential of its employees to create innovative products, provide exceptional service, and solve complex problems.

As we move further into the Age of AI, let's not forget the intrinsic human strengths that make us indispensable: the ability to observe the subtleties of the world around us, the resourcefulness to adapt and improvise, and the creativity to envision and actualize new possibilities. These qualities will continue to propel us forward, help us navigate the complex challenges ahead, and enable us to create a future that resonates with our shared human experience.

While we embrace and adapt to the Age of AI, we must continue nurturing these human values. By observing, being resourceful, and fostering creativity, we can work alongside AI and use it as a tool to complement and enhance our innate capabilities. The future is not about AI versus humans, but rather about how we can leverage the best of both to create a world that is both efficient and productive and meaningful and human.

Value 7: Efficiency and Sustainability

Our seventh value, efficiency and sustainability, forms the backbone of our approach to managing our resources and our time. We champion efficiency not as a mere buzzword but as a tool that drives our productivity and minimizes waste. It's the power behind our processes, communications, and decision-making.

Consider, for instance, the story of Jane, a project manager who used AI to simplify complex communication processes within her team. She eradicated long email threads, inefficient meetings, and conflicting schedules by integrating an AI-powered platform. The communication became seamless and efficient and allowed the team to devote their time to tasks that required their expertise. Efficiency, in this case, didn't just increase productivity, it created time – time that could be invested elsewhere.

And here is where we link back to sustainability. Sustainability is often tied to environmental considerations, which are indeed important, but it extends far beyond. Sustainability, at its core, is about endurance and maintaining the aspects of our lives that are crucial to our holistic well-being – our family, community involvement, personal growth, and even our spirituality.

Take the example of Rod, a devoted father, community leader, and software developer. By leveraging efficient AI tools at work, he significantly reduced the time he spent on mundane tasks. The hours he saved at work meant he had more time to spend with his family, invest in his local community, and engage in personal pursuits that enriched his life. That's sustainability in action, enabled by efficiency. Rod wasn't merely surviving; he was thriving in all areas of his life.

This is why it's so vital that we frame sustainability in this broader context. If we neglect any aspect of our life in the pursuit of work, in the long run, it's unsustainable. No success at work can compensate for failure in the home or a lack of personal fulfilment. True sustainability embraces all these spheres, ensuring they can continue and thrive.

Finally, the ultimate testament to sustainability is our commitment to eliminating waste in our production lines, operations, and crucially, time management. Because when we eliminate waste, we conserve our most precious commodity—time. It's efficiency that enables us to do more with the time we have, and sustainability ensures we are investing that time where it truly matters.

In an AI-driven era, the efficient use of time translates into sustainability beyond the workplace. As individuals, we must optimize efficiency to gain time, and as a society, we must encourage sustainability in all aspects of life to ensure that our success endures. Our pursuit of efficiency and sustainability isn't simply a business strategy – it's a life strategy. It is our key to a more balanced, fulfilled, and sustainable life.

Value 8: Leveraging Technology

Our eighth and final value encapsulates our commitment to leveraging technology as a means to propel our growth, enhance our efficiency, and solidify our sustainability. In the modern age, technology isn't just an add-on or a perk but a lifeline that runs through every aspect of our operations. It's a tool that powers our processes, informs our decisions, and amplifies our capabilities. But our relationship with technology is not passive; we engage with it actively, understanding it, shaping it, and directing it towards our goals.

Think about Susan, a sales manager in a mid-sized company. She saw potential in her team, but they were lagging behind due to outdated systems and manual processes. Susan advocated for an AI-powered, robust Customer Relationship Management (CRM) system. The new system automated routine tasks, provided rich customer insights and allowed the team to track sales efforts effectively. By leveraging technology, Susan didn't just improve her team's efficiency, but she also enabled them to provide a superior customer experience. Her proactive commitment to technology made all the difference.

But why is this so crucial? Why do we place such emphasis on an overt commitment to technology? In an increasingly digital world, those who fail to adapt risk not just lagging behind but being completely left behind. In the face of this risk, complacency isn't an option. A single tech laggard in a team doesn't just hold back progress, they risk the viability of the entire company. In the digital age, our survival isn't guaranteed by our present success but by our willingness to evolve and adapt to new technologies.

Consider Paul, a senior executive in a traditional logistics company. Paul was hesitant to adopt AI in streamlining the company's supply chain processes, opting instead to maintain their longstanding, manual procedures. As technological advancements transformed the industry around him, AI-powered predictive analytics, real-time tracking, and automated warehousing became industry norms. Competitors embracing these advancements began operating with far greater efficiency and precision, reducing costs, faster delivery times, and higher customer satisfaction. Despite having a base of loyal customers, Paul's company struggled to keep pace. Delays increased, costs rose, and gradually, even their most faithful clients drifted towards competitors who could offer faster and more reliable services. Paul's reluctance to leverage technology didn't merely stall his company's progress; it threatened the company's very existence.

This doesn't mean that we view technology as an end in itself. It's not about having the latest gadget or the most cutting-edge AI. It's about how we use these tools to reinforce our values and how we use them to enhance our decision-making, our efficiency, and our sustainability. The synergy of human intellect and AI isn't just about using AI to do our jobs better; it's about using AI to become better at being human, to free up our time and energy for the work that matters most.

Our commitment to leveraging technology can't be an afterthought in the new world of work. It needs to be an overt, core commitment, a promise we make to ourselves and each other. Technology underpins all of our other values; it's the backbone that supports and enhances everything we do. Without it, we risk falling behind. With it, we unlock unprecedented opportunities for growth, innovation, and success.

In the final analysis, we leverage technology not because it's trendy or expected but because it's fundamental to our survival and success. We embrace it not just as a tool but as a companion in our quest, a partner in our mission, and a catalyst for our growth.

Our Growth Manifesto Blueprint forms the lifeline for companies daring to excel in the Age of AI. This isn't a list of buzzwords or a feel-good charter. It's a survival guide, an indispensable document that shapes the DNA of a thriving organization in the AI era. These values illuminate our path, guiding us through the complex terrain of a rapidly changing technological landscape. They are more than just principles; they are a framework for action, the foundations of a future-proof company.

Consider the value of "Mutual Understanding." It's not just about understanding customers but cultivating a culture of empathy and open communication, a forum where every voice carries weight. With "Play to Win," we instil a mindset of continual improvement, not just to outpace competitors but to outdo ourselves. The "Earned Success" value stands as a beacon reminding us of the power of perseverance, acknowledging that true success is built, not bestowed.

"Customer-Centric Service" is about putting customers at the heart of everything we do, transcending transactional relationships to create lasting connections. "Honesty and Integrity" anchor us in the crucial role of trust, a non-negotiable in any business and especially vital in an AI-driven world. The value of "Observation, Resourcefulness and Creativity" prompts us to see beyond problems to discern opportunities where others only see roadblocks.

The "Efficiency and Sustainability" value advocates for lean and responsible operations, connecting high productivity with the fundamental tenet of waste elimination. And finally, "Leveraging Technology" is not about "flirting" with AI, it's about utilizing AI as a powerful tool to amplify our human capabilities and to drive our values forward.

The Growth Manifesto Blueprint is a call to action. It's an acknowledgement that our greatest asset is not AI, but our unique human potential, the very element that AI cannot replicate. By embracing this blueprint, we place humans at the helm, leveraging AI as a tool, not as an equal partner. This is the framework for sustainable growth – a world where humans, endowed with unparalleled potential and agency, use AI to manifest their vision. It's not a future where technology serves humanity but a reality where humanity, with its limitless potential, uses technology to shape the world.

MASTER AI

2

AI is transforming the world at breakneck speed, and those who grasp its mechanics will steer the change. This section is a tactical guide to mastering AI as a tool. The crux is knowledge, understanding AI's capabilities, limitations, and practical applications. Why is this indispensable? AI is akin to a double-edged sword; it can liberate or confine, depending on who wields it. Without mastering AI, you risk being manipulated or sidelined by it. However, when you dominate its functioning, you turn it into a potent tool. Whether in career, business, or personal projects, understanding AI empowers you to leverage its strengths and mitigate its weaknesses. This mastery is not just about staying relevant; it's about becoming a trailblazer in an AI-driven landscape. Equip yourself with AI acumen and turn the tides in your favour.

DOI: 10.4324/9781032684895-6

Chapter 5

A Bit of History

The Journey of Computing

Our journey in computing is a clear reflection of human inventiveness and adaptability. This journey, which began thousands of years ago with basic counting tools like the abacus, has been marked by a steady stream of innovations that have made complex calculations and data processing increasingly efficient and accessible.

The abacus, although simple, was an ingenious invention of its time, helping traders and merchants perform calculations more efficiently. However, as societies evolved, so did the need for more advanced calculation tools. This necessity for progress paved the way for innovators like Blaise Pascal and Gottfried Leibniz, who developed mechanical calculators capable of performing arithmetic at faster speeds. These inventions showcased the human capability to improve tools and solve more complex problems.

During the Industrial Revolution, human ingenuity took another leap with Charles Babbage's proposal of the Analytical Engine – a machine designed to be programmable for different tasks. Though never fully built, it represented the limitless potential of human imagination and laid the foundation for programmable computers.

The 20th century saw a rapid acceleration in computer development, fuelled by both global conflicts and an insatiable human desire for progress. During World War II, computing machines like the Z3 and Harvard Mark I were developed. Though large, these machines were powerful and instrumental in solving complex mathematical problems. The invention of electronic computers, such as

DOI: 10.4324/9781032684895-7

ENIAC and UNIVAC shortly after, represented another human achievement in shrinking size while increasing capability.

One of the pivotal moments in computing history was the invention of the transistor in the 1950s. This invention, born out of human ingenuity, allowed computers to become smaller, faster, and more energy-efficient. This set the stage for personal computers in the 1970s, drastically changing how computers were used by making them accessible to the general public.

As we entered the 21st century, the internet brought a new era of connected computing. This was a direct result of human innovation striving to make information and communication seamless. We became more connected as a global community, sharing information instantaneously and revolutionizing industries.

Today, microprocessors continue to evolve, thanks to relentless human innovation. The smartphones we use daily are a testament to how far we have come – packing immense computing power in small devices. This was made possible by the tireless efforts of engineers and scientists pushing the boundaries of what microprocessors can do.

Now we are at the dawn of the quantum computing era, another frontier being pursued by human curiosity and intellect. Though still in the early stages, quantum computing promises capabilities beyond anything we have seen before.

Throughout this journey, it is evident that the development of computing has been driven and shaped by human determination to solve problems and improve our tools. Each advancement is a chapter in the ongoing story of human capability, from the abacus to quantum computers. This ingenuity and determination will continue to forge the path of computing into the future.

The Emergence and Evolution of AI

The story of AI has been one of exciting twists and turns, driven by innovative thinkers who dared to imagine machines that could mimic human thought. Early pioneers like Charles Babbage, known as the Father of the Computer, and Alan Turing, who proposed the concept of machines that could "think," laid the foundation for AI.

Fast forward to the 1950s, when AI emerged as a scientific discipline in its own right. This was marked by the Dartmouth Workshop, where the term "AI" was first used, and its study officially began.

The growth of AI hasn't been a smooth one. It's seen periods of intense interest and research (known as AI Springs) followed by periods of decreased attention and funding (known as AI Winters). Early achievements in AI led to high expectations, and when these weren't fully met, the first AI Winter ensued in the 1970s.

The 1980s saw another AI Spring with the advent of expert systems, which tried to mimic the decision-making ability of humans. While promising, these systems had limitations, leading to another AI Winter.

The latest resurgence of AI (often called the "AI Boom") started in the late 1990s, fuelled by developments in machine learning (ML) and deep learning. With more computing power, data, and improved algorithms, AI has made major strides in areas like image and speech recognition, natural language processing, and complex games.

Today, AI is more than just a theoretical concept. It powers technologies we use every day, like self-driving cars and virtual assistants. The growth of AI is a testament to human ingenuity and persistence. While we have encountered several challenges and periods of disillusionment, each step has brought us closer to realizing the dream of creating intelligent machines.

In the early days, AI was about rule-based systems, also known as expert systems. These systems, popular in the 1970s and 1980s, tried to mimic human decision-making within a specific area of knowledge. They followed preset rules, which made them predictable but not very flexible.

These rule-based systems showed potential in areas like medical diagnosis and financial planning, where they could give advice like a human expert. But they had significant limitations. They required a lot of programming, didn't scale well, and couldn't handle uncertainty or learn from new information.

These shortcomings led researchers to look for new approaches, and this exploration led to machine learning. ML marked a big shift in AI, moving away from rigid, rule-based systems to more flexible, adaptable ones. It set the stage for the advanced AI technologies we see today.

ML, a concept introduced in 1959, has played a pivotal role in surmounting the limitations of rule-based AI systems. By learning from data rather than following explicitly programmed rules, ML algorithms have provided a more flexible and expansive approach to AI.

ML has branched into various sub-fields over the years, such as supervised, unsupervised, reinforcement (more on this in the next chapter), and deep learning. Deep learning, in particular, which uses artificial neural networks, has generated much excitement due to its success in areas like image and speech recognition, translation, and natural language processing.

This shift from rule-based systems to ML wasn't just a mere upgrade; it fundamentally transformed the nature of AI. Instead of just following a set of predefined rules, AI systems could now learn, adapt, and make decisions more autonomously. This created a myriad of new possibilities for AI, from data analysis and prediction to autonomous vehicles and personalized recommendation systems.

However, it's worth noting that ML isn't without its challenges. These include data privacy and security issues, algorithmic bias, lack of transparency, and the extensive computational resources needed to train complex models. Yet, these challenges are part and parcel of any technological evolution, similar to what we experienced during the era of rule-based systems.

As we look at the growth of AI from rule-based systems to ML, we're reminded of its incredible adaptability and progress. Every leap forward comes with new challenges, requiring ongoing research, adaptation, and innovation. This spirit of continuous discovery and problem-solving will be the driving force behind AI's foray into unexplored realms.

AI's evolution from a concept in science fiction to a powerful, transformative tool is fascinating. Key events in this journey serve as milestones, signifying the transformative power of AI. These events range from Alan Turing's profound question, "Can machines think?" in 1950, to IBM's Deep Blue defeating world chess champion Garry Kasparov in 1997, showcasing AI's potential to rival human intellect.

Subsequent landmarks such as IBM's Watson winning against Jeopardy champions in 2011, Google's AlphaGo defeating world Go champion Lee Sedol in 2016, and the advent of AI-powered virtual assistants like Siri, Alexa, and Google Assistant have shown the world just how far AI has come. Not to forget the development of autonomous vehicles by companies like Tesla and Waymo, which stands as a testament to AI's transformative potential in the transportation sector.

These milestones in AI's development, from Turing's test to Deep Blue's victory, Watson's language understanding, AlphaGo's strategic capabilities, and the integration of AI in everyday life through virtual assistants and self-driving cars, give us a clear view of AI's evolution. They help us understand where AI has been, where it stands today, and its exciting potential for the future.

But it's important to remember that this story isn't over. AI continues to evolve and mature, and we can anticipate more milestones that will continue redefining our understanding of what's possible with this technology.

The Basic Mechanics of AI

AI is currently powered by a host of advanced technologies, including deep learning, a subfield of ML. Deep learning uses complex algorithms and neural networks to make significant strides in what machines can achieve.

Deep learning models learn from a wealth of data, using artificial neural networks with multiple hidden layers, thus the term "deep." These models can process data in complex, non-linear ways, attempting to emulate human decision-making. They extract features in a layered manner, starting from simple to more sophisticated attributes.

One of the main tools in AI today is convolutional neural networks (CNNs), particularly useful for processing visual data. CNNs are used in applications like image recognition, helping identify friends in social media photos or aiding self-driving cars to "see" their surroundings.

Another key development in AI is recurrent neural networks (RNNs), designed to handle sequential data. RNNs remember previous inputs in a sequence, making them ideal for tasks like speech recognition, language modelling, and translation. When you voice a text message on your phone or chat with a bot, it's likely an RNN at work.

RNNs have taken a major leap forward by introducing long short-term memory (LSTM) networks. These networks can learn from long sequences without the usual information decay over time, making them crucial for tasks like music generation, text production, and stock price prediction.

Generative adversarial networks (GANs) are also shaping today's AI landscape. These networks generate realistic content, from images to music, sparking both creativity and ethical debates.

Reinforcement learning, where an AI agent learns through trial and error, is another critical part of AI today. This learning style has driven breakthroughs like AlphaGo's victory over a human champion and continues progressing AI in games and beyond.

It's important to remember that we are only at the beginning. Despite our incredible strides, we have barely scratched the surface of what is possible with this transformative technology.

CNNs enable facial recognition in our social media apps and help self-driving cars "see" their surroundings. Yet, the most advanced CNN still does not match the human eye's ability to quickly interpret complex visual scenes. Our brains effortlessly understand context and subtle emotional cues and interpret abstract art – capabilities that continue to elude CNNs.

RNNs, with their ability to process sequential data, are behind many language-processing and speech-recognition technologies. They're integral to our digital assistants and predictive text functions. But, compare this to the nuanced understanding of language, the ability to appreciate poetry or understand sarcasm, that a human possesses. RNNs have a long way to go.

GNNs, essential for understanding and working with complex systems, are another area where AI has made significant advances but is still far from human abilities. GNNs can analyse social networks or molecular structures, but humans effortlessly navigate the complex networks of social interactions, understanding unspoken rules and adjusting to new social situations – a level of understanding currently out of reach for GNNs.

Yes, AI has come a long way, but we are still at the dawn of what is possible. As we develop more advanced algorithms and our machines learn from ever-increasing data, AI capabilities will continue to grow. The future holds untold possibilities, from fully autonomous vehicles to AI systems that better mimic understanding while interacting more with the world.

This exploration into the world of AI isn't a sprint but a marathon. It's a quest of ongoing discovery, constant learning, and persistent innovation. As we push the boundaries of what AI can achieve, we'll continue to enhance our lives, transform our industries, and open up new horizons for human capabilities. Despite our significant advances, we are just beginning to explore the vast potential of AI. It's an exciting time, and we are at the forefront of this incredible adventure.

The foundational principle of AI is its capacity to learn from experience, a mechanism made possible by the crucial role of data. This learning model is the cornerstone of AI technology. This part of the book delves into the intricacies of this fundamental principle, the centrality of data in AI, and how ML algorithms utilize this to improve over time.

Data is the lifeblood of AI. It provides the crucial context, insights, and experiential understanding that AI relies on to learn and make decisions. Just as humans learn and evolve based on experiences, AI systems use data as their experience. ML, a core subset of AI, thrives on the availability of quality data. This data provides the context necessary for the system to discern patterns, predict trends, and make informed decisions.

Take, for instance, recommendation systems used by platforms such as Netflix or Amazon. These systems meticulously analyse user-specific data – viewing history, product preferences, and shopping patterns – alongside similar data from other users. ML algorithms identify patterns within this data, utilizing it to predict future user preferences and deliver personalized recommendations.

Self-driving cars provide another illustrative example. Through cameras and sensors, these vehicles continuously collect vast amounts of data about their environment – traffic conditions, pedestrian movements, other vehicles, and much more. This data is processed in real-time, enabling the car to make safety-critical decisions on the go. Furthermore, the data collected over time helps improve the vehicle's future performance.

Deep learning, introduced as an advanced subset of ML, employs artificial neural networks to learn from unstructured and unlabelled data. This capability enables it to master tasks such as image and speech recognition, natural language processing, and creative endeavours such as composing original music or generating artwork. All these functions underscore the transformative potential of data in AI.

However, the reliance on data also raises challenges and concerns. The questions of data privacy, security, and bias are becoming increasingly prominent. If an AI system is trained on biased or unrepresentative data, it can perpetuate and even exacerbate those biases. As such, responsible and ethical data handling is critical to ensuring AI's fair and equitable application.

In sum, data is the fuel that propels AI systems, providing the experiential input they learn and evolve from. As we continue to navigate an increasingly data-driven world, understanding the integral role of data in AI and the principle of learning from experience is paramount. This foundation will allow us to leverage AI responsibly and effectively in our careers, businesses, and personal lives. The forthcoming bits will build on this fundamental understanding, exploring the other critical principles that underpin AI.

One of the most intriguing facets of AI is its capacity for reasoning and problem-solving, a quality that has earned it the moniker of the "thinking machine." In this realm, AI demonstrates an uncanny ability to mimic a crude form of human responses.

The ability of AI to solve problems is founded on rule-based systems, a principle that harkens back to the early days of AI. Rule-based systems operate on predefined "if–then" logic, providing a direct, deterministic approach to problem-solving. For instance, consider an AI system programmed to play chess. The system would operate on a series of rules like, "If the opponent's queen threatens your king, then move the king to a safe square." Such rules offer a clear action pathway based on a given condition, allowing AI to make decisions and execute actions.

Yet, these rule-based systems are not without their shortcomings. A rule-based system is entirely dependent on the rules pre-programmed by human coders, limiting its flexibility. Furthermore, such systems struggle with situations of ambiguity, an area where a human excels with its ability to consider context and nuance.

The advent of ML marked a significant leap in the development of AI's reasoning capabilities. Instead of rigidly adhering to hard-coded rules, AI systems can now learn from experience, much like a human would. This shift to experiential learning allows AI to discern patterns, absorb feedback, and make increasingly autonomous decisions.

Picture an AI system designed to distinguish between photos of dogs and cats. Rather than programming exhaustive rules for every conceivable breed and variation, ML algorithms allow the system to learn from a dataset of labelled images. Over time, this AI system can accurately categorize new images without human intervention.

However, as the reasoning capabilities of AI continue to evolve and become more complex, so too do the challenges that researchers face. One such issue is the "black box" phenomenon, where the decision-making process of an AI system is opaque and difficult to interpret. Despite the challenge it presents, it also catalyses further research and innovation, pushing us towards developing AI systems that are not only effective but also transparent in their operations.

AI's progress in emulating human-like reasoning is an ongoing endeavour. Through applying principles like rule-based systems and ML, AI continues to edge closer to mimicking human intellectual capabilities. Every breakthrough brings us a step closer to a future where AI's reasoning and problem-solving abilities augment and enhance our own, propelling us towards new horizons of discovery and innovation.

As a summary, AI has drastically transformed our interaction with technology. One aspect of AI that's especially remarkable is its ability to perceive and understand its environment, enabling it to interact with the world to a far greater degree than any time before.

The realm of computer vision is a notable example of AI's perception abilities. Computer vision allows machines to "see" and interpret visual data, opening avenues for countless applications, from facial recognition systems to self-driving cars. Consider how a self-driving car uses computer vision to navigate its environment. It relies on cameras and sensors to capture visual data, identifying road signs, pedestrians, and other vehicles. These visual cues are interpreted and used to make decisions like when to slow down, speed up, or change lanes.

This understanding of the world isn't limited to sight. Natural language processing (NLP), another critical AI domain, allows machines to comprehend and generate human language. This field of AI is at the core of various services we use daily – think about voice assistants like Alexa or Siri that respond to voice commands or email filters that separate spam from important messages. They utilize NLP to understand the intricacies of human language, identifying and interpreting the meaning, context, and sentiment of words and phrases.

AI can interpret ultraviolet or infrared visual data, see through walls with Wi-Fi signals, or process vast datasets quickly and accurately – things that humans don't need to do. This gives AI a unique purpose in fields like healthcare, where it can analyse medical images to detect diseases in their early stages, or in astronomy, where it can process cosmic images to identify new celestial bodies.

However, AI's interpretation of the world is far from flawless. AI systems struggle with tasks that humans find intuitive. These result from AI's inherent limitations – they lack the broader context of the world, the nuanced understanding of situations, and the shared cultural knowledge that humans possess.

Even with the promising advancements and the capabilities AI has shown, it is important to realize that we are still in the early stages of this technological advance. As remarkable as AI's problem-solving abilities may appear, they are currently limited by the quality and quantity of the data they learn from, their programming, and our still-developing understanding of the technology.

Comparing AI to human intellect, even at its most advanced stage, AI is outmatched by a human's apparently infinite cognitive abilities. For instance, a human child can understand and learn from ambiguities, inconsistencies, and incomplete information in a way that current AI systems cannot. Humans can also apply learned knowledge to new, unseen scenarios flexibly and intuitively – a characteristic known as generalization. This ability is currently beyond the grasp of AI.

Moreover, it's important to note that while AI has made leaps in emulating minuscule facets of human thinking and perception, these are still far from complete. Tasks that humans perform intuitively, like recognizing familiar faces in different contexts or understanding humour, often present a significant challenge to AI. In this regard, the intelligence of even a young child is remarkably flexible and adaptable compared to the most advanced AI systems of today.

In essence, while AI has demonstrated the potential to mimic minor aspects of human ability, it's crucial to understand that these systems do not possess the rich, nuanced, and flexible intellect inherent to humans. As we continue to explore and push the boundaries of AI, it is our responsibility to approach this powerful technology with a balanced perspective, leveraging its capabilities and respecting its current limitations.

Chapter 6

Coming to Terms with What AI Can and Cannot Do

Types and Techniques of AI

Machine learning (ML) models use algorithms to receive input data, learn patterns within the data, and make decisions or predictions based on those patterns. It's like a child learning to recognize dogs – with exposure to various breeds, sizes, and colours of dogs, the child learns the commonalities that make a dog a dog.

As mentioned in the previous chapter, there are three important types of machine learning: supervised, unsupervised, and reinforcement learning.

Supervised learning is akin to learning with a teacher. It involves training an algorithm on a labelled dataset – a dataset where the desired outcome is known. For instance, an email spam filter is a classic example of supervised learning. The algorithm is trained on a set of emails that are labelled as "spam" or "not spam," and learns to classify new emails based on the patterns it recognized during training. The "supervision" comes from the correct answers the algorithm learns from during training.

In contrast, unsupervised learning is like learning through exploration. The algorithm is given an unlabelled dataset and must find patterns or relationships in the data on its own. A common use case for unsupervised learning is customer segmentation in marketing. The algorithm groups customers based on

DOI: 10.4324/9781032684895-8

their behaviour or characteristics without being explicitly told what these groups should be.

Reinforcement learning, meanwhile, is learning through trial and error, like a player in a game. In this context, the algorithm, often called an agent, learns to make decisions by performing actions and receiving rewards or penalties. The agent seeks to maximize the rewards over time, adjusting its strategy based on the feedback it receives. This type of learning powers Google's AlphaGo, the first AI to beat a world champion Go player.

Despite their differences, all types of ML share a common goal: to learn from data to make accurate predictions or decisions. As the algorithms learn more and more from the data they process, their performance improves.

However, ML also has its limitations and challenges. The quality of the predictions depends largely on the quality of the data it learns from. Poor data can lead to poor predictions. Moreover, ML models can make it difficult to understand how they've made their decisions. This raises ethical issues, especially in sensitive applications like healthcare or criminal justice.

ML is a fascinating path of continuous learning and improvement. As we feed it more data and refine its algorithms, ML becomes increasingly capable of astounding feats, from detecting diseases in medical images to driving cars. It opens a world of possibilities, allowing machines to learn, adapt, and make decisions, profoundly changing how we live and work.

Deep learning stands at the forefront of modern AI. This computational model, inspired by the idea of biological neural networks, allows machines to mimic our ability to learn from experience, understand complex patterns, and make nuanced decisions. The magic of deep learning lies in its capacity to handle vast amounts of data and create sophisticated representations of the world.

Neural networks, the backbone of deep learning, consist of interconnected layers of nodes, often called neurons or units. These networks process data by transmitting it through the layers, with each layer learning to extract features and patterns that contribute to the final output or decision. This layered approach allows neural networks to learn complex patterns in large datasets, making deep learning particularly effective for tasks like image recognition, natural language processing, etc.

A key strength of neural networks is their ability to learn hierarchical representations, meaning lower layers learn simple features (like lines or colours in an image), while deeper layers combine these simple features to learn more complex representations (like shapes, objects, or even faces).

Let's delve deeper into the structure of a typical neural network. It consists of an input layer, one or more hidden layers, and an output layer. The input layer receives raw data, such as the pixel values of an image. Each neuron in the hidden layer processes a part of the data, learning a specific feature or pattern. The output layer produces the final decision, such as classifying an image.

The neurons in a neural network are connected via synapses. Each is assigned a "weight" that determines the strength of the connection. During the training phase, these weights are adjusted based on the error of the network's output. This is achieved through a process known as backpropagation, a technique that adjusts the weights of the connections to minimize the difference between the network's predictions and the actual results.

Returning to the discussion of the different neural networks, convolutional neural networks (CNNs) use filters to scan input data for specific features, significantly reducing the number of parameters needed and thus making the network more efficient. Recurrent neural networks (RNNs) have a unique feature that allows them to retain information from previous inputs in the sequence, giving them a form of memory.

However, deep learning also faces challenges. These networks require vast amounts of data to train effectively and significant computational resources as well. Additionally, their decision-making process can be hard to interpret, raising issues of transparency and accountability.

Deep learning and neural networks represent a significant leap in the evolution of AI. They have transformed industries, providing unparalleled capabilities in areas like automated translation, voice recognition, autonomous driving, and more. As we refine these tools and understand their potential, we expect to see even more revolutionary changes in our digital landscape.

Natural language processing (NLP) serves as a critical bridge between humans and machines, enabling our digital companions to comprehend, interpret, and generate human language. This multidisciplinary field draws from computer science, linguistics, and cognitive science to create algorithms that navigate language's delicate structures, nuances, and ambiguities.

At its core, NLP aims to transform unstructured text data, replete with context, idioms, and complex grammar, into structured data that computers can understand and analyse. This ambitious goal involves numerous tasks, ranging from simple ones, such as tokenization (breaking down text into individual words or "tokens") and part-of-speech tagging (identifying the grammatical role of each word), to complex ones, like semantic analysis (understanding the meaning of sentences) and sentiment analysis (detecting emotional tones in text).

To appreciate the depth of NLP, consider machine translation, a widely used NLP application. Simple word-for-word translation is insufficient to capture the subtleties and context of the source language. Instead, NLP algorithms, particularly those based on deep learning, parse the text, capture its meaning, and then generate the translation, maintaining the essence of the original content.

NLP's transformative power is also evident in chatbots and virtual assistants like Siri, Alexa, and Google Assistant. These applications employ NLP to understand spoken or written commands, generate human-like responses, and even anticipate user needs based on past interactions. This process involves understanding syntax (the arrangement of words), semantics (the meaning of words and sentences), and pragmatics (the use of language in different contexts).

However, teaching machines to understand human language is far from straightforward. Each language has its own idiosyncrasies, and within each language, dialects, slang, and cultural references add another layer of complexity. Beyond that, human communication is rich with implicit meaning and context, often conveyed through tone, body language, or shared cultural knowledge. These nuances pose substantial challenges for NLP.

Recent advancements, however, have significantly improved NLP's capabilities. A pivotal breakthrough was the development of transformer-based models like Google's Bidirectional Encoder Representations from Transformers (BERT) and OpenAI's Generative Pretrained Transformer (GPT). These models leverage context from previous and following words in a sentence, resulting in a far more nuanced understanding of language.

BERT, for instance, revolutionized the field with its ability to consider the full context of a word by looking at the words that come before and after it. This approach improved the model's performance in several NLP tasks, including question answering, named entity recognition, and sentiment analysis.

On the other hand, GPT models demonstrated impressive language-generation capabilities. GPT-4 can generate coherent and contextually relevant sentences, creating human-like text that has often been hard to distinguish from text written by a person.

Despite these advancements, challenges persist. The complexity of deep learning models hinders interpretability, a crucial factor for applications in sensitive domains like healthcare or law. Moreover, the models require vast amounts of annotated training data, which can be resource-intensive to gather and maintain.

Despite these challenges, NLP holds immense potential. As we refine our methods, we're moving closer to a future where natural, intuitive interaction between humans and machines becomes the norm, opening new frontiers in technology and society. From facilitating real-time translation to empowering visually impaired individuals with text-to-speech services, NLP is shaping the future of human–computer interaction.

Real-World Applications of AI

AI is revolutionizing the healthcare field by enhancing diagnostics, treatment planning, patient care, and drug discovery, underscoring the transformative power of smart algorithms in saving lives.

AI's impact on healthcare is pervasive, transcending disciplines and specialities. In diagnostics, ML algorithms are proving adept at analysing medical images. Radiology, for instance, has been dramatically transformed by the advent of AI. Deep learning models can analyse CT scans, MRIs, and X-rays, often matching or even surpassing the accuracy of human experts in detecting anomalies such as tumours or fractures. These AI systems can also identify patterns that may be overlooked by the human eye, thereby improving the early detection of diseases.

In addition, AI is making strides in pathology, where it's used to identify and classify diseases in tissue samples. PathAI, a leading company dedicated to improving patient outcomes with reliable AI-powered technology, has developed algorithms that assist pathologists in diagnosing diseases more accurately and quickly. This automation enhances diagnostic accuracy and helps address the global shortage of pathologists.

AI's impact extends beyond diagnostics into predictive analytics, where algorithms analyse vast patient data to predict health outcomes. This ability is especially valuable in managing chronic conditions like diabetes or heart disease, where early intervention can dramatically improve patient outcomes.

Moreover, AI is revolutionizing patient care and management. AI-powered virtual assistants and chatbots provide patients with instant medical advice, reminders for medication, and personalized health tips. These applications enhance patient engagement, adherence to treatment plans, and overall health outcomes.

The advent of wearable devices has further expanded AI's role in patient care. These devices collect real-time health data like heart rate, sleep patterns, and physical activity. AI algorithms can analyse these data to monitor patient health, provide personalized feedback, and alert healthcare providers of alarming trends.

Furthermore, AI is significantly impacting drug discovery and development, an area traditionally characterized by high costs and long timelines. AI algorithms can analyse vast biomedical databases, predict how different compounds will interact with the body, and suggest potential drug candidates. By accelerating the drug discovery process, AI saves time and resources and facilitates the development of treatments for diseases that currently have none.

In the face of the COVID-19 pandemic, AI demonstrated its power by aiding in various aspects of the crisis. AI tools were used to track the spread of the virus, identify high-risk individuals, analyse public health data, and speed up vaccine development. Such applications highlighted the potential of AI as a crucial tool in pandemic response and preparedness.

Despite these promising developments, the implementation of AI in healthcare faces challenges. Data privacy is a significant concern, given the sensitive nature of health information. In addition, the complex nature of AI algorithms raises transparency and trust issues. Ensuring the fairness and bias-free performance of AI models is also crucial, particularly in healthcare, where the stakes are high.

Moreover, the integration of AI into healthcare requires changes in workflows, which could meet resistance from healthcare professionals. Educating clinicians about AI's benefits and limitations is essential for fostering acceptance and encouraging effective use.

As these challenges are addressed, the benefits of AI in healthcare will likely continue to multiply. The future of healthcare holds a vision of personalized medicine, where AI algorithms, armed with genomic data and real-time health metrics, will tailor treatments to individual patients, improving the effectiveness of treatments and enhancing patient outcomes.

The progress of AI in healthcare is just beginning. As the field continues to evolve, the symbiosis of AI and human intelligence promises a future where healthcare is more accurate, efficient, and personalized.

Beyond healthcare, AI is a contemporary reality influencing how businesses operate and innovate, redefining customer service, optimizing logistics, enhancing marketing, and creating new paths for profitability.

In the realm of customer service, AI has brought an unprecedented shift. AI-powered chatbots and virtual assistants are now ubiquitous, handling customer inquiries 24/7 and providing immediate responses. The advanced natural language processing capabilities of these AI tools allow them to understand customer queries, provide accurate responses, and learn from each interaction to improve future responses. This enhances customer satisfaction and frees up human agents to handle complex issues, thereby improving operational efficiency.

Outside customer interaction, AI is powering personalized marketing campaigns. By analysing vast amounts of customer data, AI can identify patterns, predict consumer behaviour, and tailor marketing content to individual preferences.

In the logistics and supply chain domain, AI optimizes operations in numerous ways. AI-powered predictive analytics can forecast demand more accurately, helping businesses manage inventory efficiently and reduce costs associated with overstocking or stockouts. AI algorithms can also optimize delivery routes, considering factors such as traffic, weather, and vehicle capacity, reducing fuel consumption and delivery times.

Moreover, AI is aiding in strategic decision-making through advanced data analysis. ML algorithms can analyse complex datasets, identify trends and patterns, and generate insights that inform business strategies. This application of AI is especially valuable in areas such as financial forecasting, risk management, and market analysis.

AI also plays a significant role in human resources, where it automates repetitive tasks, such as resume screening and scheduling interviews. AI-powered tools can analyse job descriptions and resumes to match candidates with suitable jobs, reducing the time-to-hire and enhancing the quality of hires. Furthermore, AI can aid in employee engagement and retention by identifying patterns in employee behaviour and feedback, helping HR teams to develop strategies to improve workplace satisfaction.

Furthermore, AI is creating new business opportunities by developing AI-based products and services. Tech giants like Google, Amazon, and Microsoft offer AI capabilities as a service, allowing businesses of all sizes to leverage AI without investing in expensive infrastructure. Start-ups are innovating with AI in numerous fields, from healthcare and education to finance and entertainment, creating a vibrant and competitive AI ecosystem.

However, the implementation of AI in business is not without challenges. Businesses must navigate issues related to data privacy and security, algorithmic bias, and the potential displacement of jobs due to automation. This is exacerbated by the attendant impact on workplace culture brought to bear by these issues. Moreover, integrating AI into existing business processes requires strategic planning, investment, and change management.

As businesses strive to overcome these challenges, the transformative power of AI in business becomes more apparent. The possibilities for improved efficiency, innovation, and profitability are extensive, and the businesses that can effectively leverage AI will likely gain a competitive edge in the increasingly digital and data-driven business landscape.

Looking to the future, the evolution of AI promises even more exciting possibilities for business. The development of AI technologies such as autonomous vehicles, quantum computing, and advanced robotics holds the promise of new business models and industry transformations. As AI continues to evolve and mature, it will remain a driving force behind business innovation and profitability.

Ultimately, the rise of AI in business signals a paradigm shift in how businesses operate and innovate. The businesses that embrace this shift and effectively leverage AI's potential stand to reap substantial benefits, including improved operational efficiency, enhanced customer satisfaction, and increased profitability.

The impact of AI is not limited to the confines of the laboratory and the corporate world. It is reshaping our everyday lives. AI's influence is pervasive and profound, from smart home devices and personal assistants to self-driving cars and beyond.

The past decade has witnessed a swift influx of AI-powered technologies into our homes, changing our domestic landscape forever. Smart home devices like Amazon's Echo with Alexa, Google Home, and Apple's HomeKit are leading this transformation. Armed with AI capabilities, these devices are transforming how we interact with our environment. They respond to our voice commands, control home appliances, play our favourite music, give us news and weather updates, and even order groceries. They're always learning, adapting to our routines, and becoming more efficient at anticipating our needs.

Smart home devices also contribute to home security. AI-powered security cameras and systems can recognize faces, distinguish between pets and potential intruders, and alert homeowners to unusual activity. Meanwhile, AI-enabled thermostats like Google's Nest learn our schedules and comfort preferences to manage heating and cooling more efficiently, conserving energy, and saving money.

AI's impact doesn't stop at our front doors. It extends into the open road with autonomous vehicles. Companies like Tesla, Waymo, and Uber are pioneering self-driving technology, revolutionizing our concept of personal transportation. These vehicles rely on AI to navigate, make split-second decisions, and learn from each journey. As AI continues to mature, we can expect autonomous vehicles to become a common sight, promising safer roads, fewer traffic jams, and more leisure time for individuals.

However, it's not just our physical lives that AI is reshaping. AI personal assistants like Apple's Siri, Microsoft's Cortana, and Google Assistant are making our digital interactions more seamless. They help us manage our schedules, answer queries, send messages, and even make reservations. They're becoming our personal concierges, making life easier and more organized.

As we stand on the threshold of a new AI-driven era, it's clear that the applications of AI in our personal lives will continue to grow. We're moving towards a future where our homes will become smarter, our cars will drive themselves, and AI will become an even more integrated part of our everyday lives, offering convenience, efficiency, and a touch of the future, today.

These examples just scratch the surface of AI's potential. As research and development in AI continue, we can expect even more disruptions and transformations. However, this comes with challenges. Businesses must adapt to fast changes, regulations must address new ethical and security issues, and individuals must learn new skills for the AI-driven economy.

Understanding AI today, its capabilities, and its limitations, is essential for navigating this transformative time. This will help you adapt, thrive, and potentially shape this exciting new frontier of human innovation.

The Limitations of AI

AI is transforming industries and societies with its ability to analyse vast amounts of data, make accurate predictions, and automate complex tasks. However, it's essential to consider the other side of the coin. Despite its monumental achieve-ments, AI has limitations and faces significant challenges.

One of the most prominent limitations of current AI systems is their lack of common-sense reasoning. AI algorithms excel at pattern recognition and making predictions based on historical data. Yet, they struggle with tasks that humans find trivial, like understanding the physical properties of objects or inferring the intentions of others. The world makes sense to humans because we possess common sense – an intuitive understanding of how things work. We know, for instance, that water is wet without having to touch it or that an object dropped will fall due to gravity. AI, however, lacks this innate understanding.

Deep learning algorithms, which are at the forefront of modern AI, can make sense of complex patterns in data, but they often fail to understand the context. They are trained to map inputs to outputs but often miss the "why" behind these mappings. For example, an image-recognition AI might accurately label a picture of a dog in a living room as a "dog." However, it wouldn't com-prehend that the room is a living space, the dog is a pet, or that pets are usually kept for companionship.

Another challenge is the need for large amounts of data. Machine learning models require vast data sets to train effectively. Collecting and curating these datasets can be resource-intensive. Furthermore, the reliance on historical data can also lead to models that perpetuate and amplify existing biases present in the data. For instance, an AI system used in hiring might favour certain demo-graphics if past hiring decisions showed a preference for those groups.

AI's difficulty in explaining its decision-making process problem is another considerable challenge. While AI can outperform humans in tasks ranging from image recognition to game playing, it often can't explain its decisions clearly. This lack of interpretability and transparency is a significant concern in high-stakes domains like healthcare or criminal justice, where understanding the rationale behind decisions is crucial.

AI is also brittle in the sense that slight changes in the input data can cause significant changes in output, which a human would not consider reasonable. This lack of robustness to small agitations makes AI systems susceptible to adversarial attacks – deliberate attempts to fool the AI.

AI systems currently lack the ability to effectively transfer learning from one context to another. While a human can apply knowledge learned in one domain to a related one, AI struggles with this. Each new task often requires starting from scratch, collecting a new dataset, and spending significant resources on retraining.

While researchers are actively working on these issues, they serve as a sober-ing reminder that despite the rapid progress in AI, there is still a long way to go. The path to more capable, robust, and broadly applicable AI will require us to refine and enhance current methods and develop new approaches that address these foundational challenges. Understanding these limitations and their challenges is a critical step in this process, ensuring we approach the AI revolution with a balanced and informed perspective.

AI has made significant strides, achieving feats previously considered the exclusive domain of human intellect. But AI is not human, and this distinction is critical to understanding the interaction between humans and AI and recognizing the unique value of human intelligence.

To begin with, it's crucial to remember that AI is a tool designed, built, and deployed by humans to accomplish specific tasks. It does not possess consciousness or emotions, and it doesn't have desires or intentions. AI does not "think" like humans do; it follows algorithms and uses statistical analysis to find patterns and make predictions.

Human intelligence, on the other hand, is holistic and multifaceted. It includes rationality and logic, certainly, but also creativity, emotional intelligence, moral judgement, intuition, and a sense of self-awareness. These aspects of intelligence enable humans to understand complex and nuanced situations, engage in deep conversation, form meaningful relationships, appreciate art, and create new things.

Creativity is one area where human intelligence shines brightly. AI can generate new content based on learned patterns, but it doesn't truly create in the human sense. It doesn't come up with novel ideas that diverge from the data it was trained on. Humans, in contrast, can produce original works of art, literature, music, and scientific theory that go beyond what has been seen or done before.

Emotional intelligence is another realm where humans outstrip AI. While AI can recognize patterns indicating emotions in text or speech, it doesn't experience emotions and cannot empathize with others genuinely. Humans, with their capacity for empathy and understanding, are crucial for tasks that require emotional sensitivity, such as counselling or social work.

Additionally, moral and ethical judgement is a uniquely human capacity. While researchers are developing techniques for "ethical AI" and "fairness in ML," AI's understanding of ethics fundamentally differs from human morality. It relies on coded guidelines and learned patterns rather than an internalized sense of right and wrong. Decisions with ethical implications, from healthcare to legal judgements, still require a human touch.

AI's lack of self-awareness and consciousness is also a significant difference. AI does not have a sense of self or subjective experience. It doesn't "want" to win a game of Go – it plays the game because it was programmed to do so. This lack of consciousness means AI doesn't have needs, rights, or desires, unlike humans.

Humans are also indispensable in designing, training, and overseeing AI. Machine learning algorithms need to be trained on data that is collected and labelled by humans. Human expertise is needed to ensure that AI is performing correctly, to interpret the results it produces, and to decide when, where, and how to deploy AI systems.

Finally, humans are uniquely equipped to deal with novel situations and challenges. While AI excels in environments with clear rules and abundant data, it struggles in unfamiliar situations. Humans, with their ability to generalize from past experiences and apply knowledge in new contexts, can adapt and innovate when faced with the unexpected.

While AI has proven to be an extraordinarily powerful tool capable of tasks that augment human capabilities, it does not replace human intelligence. The blend of rational, creative, emotional, moral, and intuitive aspects of human intelligence remains unparalleled and indispensable. As we continue to develop and deploy AI, it's important to remember the unique strengths of human intelligence and ensure that we leverage AI in ways that benefit humanity rather than attempting to replicate or replace our innate abilities.

One of the most significant challenges facing AI today is bias. Bias in AI, unintentional though it may be, can result in unfair outcomes, from skewed hiring decisions to biased law enforcement practices. In essence, the task is to ensure that AI respects and promotes fairness and equality.

AI systems learn from data, and if this data carries societal biases, these can be replicated and even amplified in AI systems. Consider an AI tool for resume screening trained on a dataset of successful hires from a tech company. If most of those successful hires were men, the AI might implicitly learn that being male is a factor associated with being a good fit for the company, leading to bias against female applicants.

Another source of bias is in the AI design process itself. The teams that design AI systems are not always diverse, and this lack of diversity can lead to blind spots where certain groups' needs and perspectives are overlooked. For example, a speech recognition system designed primarily by native English speakers might perform poorly on accents not represented in the design team.

So, how can we mitigate bias in AI? Firstly, by acknowledging that it exists. Only by recognizing and accepting that AI systems can perpetuate bias can we begin to address the problem. Secondly, we can strive for diversity and inclusion in the teams that design and build AI systems. A diverse team is more likely to spot potential biases and address them before they become embedded in AI systems.

Thirdly, we need to focus on data. Data is the lifeblood of AI and ensuring that the data is unbiased is critical. This might involve collecting more diverse data or adjusting data so that it better represents the problem space. In some cases, it may also involve transparency about the data's origins and potential limitations.

In addition to data, the design of the AI model itself can also be adjusted. Techniques such as fairness-aware ML algorithms have been developed to directly reduce bias in AI predictions. These techniques modify the learning process to promote fairness by ensuring that the AI performs equally well for different demographic groups.

Transparency and explainability in AI can also help mitigate bias. If we understand how an AI system is making its decisions, we can better identify and address bias. Methods are being developed to make AI systems more interpretable, allowing us to see which factors are influencing AI decisions.

Regulation and guidelines around AI and bias also play an essential role. Various institutions and governments are developing guidelines to ensure that AI systems are fair and unbiased. For example, the EU has proposed regulations requiring high-risk AI systems to provide transparency about functioning and undergo bias checks.

Finally, ongoing monitoring and auditing of AI systems can help identify and address bias. Even after an AI system is deployed, it should be regularly tested to ensure it performs fairly as new data comes in. Overcoming bias in AI is not a one-time task but an ongoing process of vigilance, adjustment, and learning. As AI becomes more ingrained in our society, the importance of tackling this challenge only increases. Ensuring that AI systems are fair and unbiased is not just a technical issue but a societal one, critical for building an equitable future where AI benefits all.

Chapter 7

AI as a Transformative Productivity Hack

Let's Zero-In on You

As we steer through this chapter, "AI as a Transformative Productivity Hack," the spotlight is trained on you. Before we delve into how AI can augment our productivity, let's first acknowledge and leverage the arenas where human capabilities eclipse anything artificial intelligence can conjure. As we expose these areas, we'll see how our abilities shape AI's potential as a productivity amplifier.

A trait humans possess in abundance, and something AI cannot replicate, is the ability to observe keenly and reflect deeply. As exemplified in Chapter 3, the erosion of the Washington Monument was an enigmatic problem which revealed its roots through keen observation and enquiry. The alertness to question why the erosion was occurring, rather than presuming material flaws, unveiled the reality of an external factor – the lights being turned on too early, leading to the use of harsh chemicals for cleaning. By turning the lights on later, a simple and elegant solution was found. This exemplifies how keen observation can lead to unexpected insights and practical resolutions.

Observation in the age of AI takes a new turn. It involves keenly understanding AI's operations and outcomes, questioning its decisions, and discerning any biases. Through our vigilant watch, we can ensure AI tools work in our best interests and enhance productivity rather than becoming vehicles of flawed decision-making.

 DOI: 10.4324/9781032684895-9

Humans excel in building and nurturing relationships. It's an innate skill honed over centuries as we formed tribes, societies, and civilizations. We thrive in social environments, understanding and empathizing with one another, skills AI is yet to master fully. In the professional arena, building strong relationships can make a critical difference. The rapport we build with our team, customers, and partners propels us forward.

When we integrate AI into our interpersonal dynamics, the result can be truly transformative. AI can analyse patterns, streamline communication, even predict behaviours, but the finesse of human interaction is the touchstone that forms genuine connections.

Human capacity for problem-solving is another domain where we reign supreme. We solve problems in a contextual, nuanced manner, with the understanding of subtleties, cultural variances, and emotional undertones, elements that still baffle AI. We draw from our personal experiences and empathetic understanding to devise solutions that are effective and resonate at a human level.

As we harness AI's analytical prowess, it becomes our partner in problem-solving, crunching data at unprecedented speed and accuracy, giving us insights that inform our decisions. Yet, our nuanced, empathetic understanding breathes life into these solutions.

Humans are wired for communication, capable of conveying complex ideas, invoking strong emotions, or persuading a listener with articulate arguments. Our words are often interlaced with subtle meanings, insinuations, and emotional tones, nuances lost on AI.

In our interactions with AI, our human communication skills become the bridge between complex technology and meaningful application. We are the poets and narrators who can translate the language of AI, help others understand it, and ensure it serves our collective good.

Creativity, the power to birth ideas, is a uniquely human endeavour. As highlighted in Chapter 3, every man-made object began as a spark in a human mind. Even with AI's astounding strides, it remains a tool entirely dependent on our input for original thought.

Creativity in the realm of AI can birth ingenious solutions, marry human imagination with AI's processing power, and create a symphony of innovation that propels productivity. Let's celebrate our ability to express nuanced preferences, something far superior to anything AI can simulate. Whether it's cooking a meal, writing a poem, composing a melody, or simply choosing a colour palette.

As we enter a new era defined by rapid technological advancements, the Age of Agency, it's crucial to understand and embrace a novel concept called the Zone of Opportunity. This zone represents a unique intersection between AI's limitations and human capabilities. It's the sweet spot where human intuition, creativity, and adaptability meet the realms that AI is yet to conquer or may never fully master. Identifying and immersing oneself in this zone is not just a pathway to personal and professional success but a call for human ingenuity to thrive in harmony with AI.

The Zone of Opportunity is where our human agency blossoms and empowers us to carve out spaces and create value that AI alone cannot achieve. Our ability to find and capitalize on this zone is vital for staying relevant, innovative, and indispensable in a world that increasingly relies on algorithms. Now, let's delve into the specifics of AI vulnerabilities and explore how, as humans, we can turn them into avenues of opportunity.

To future-proof our careers in the age of AI, we need to understand not just the general limitations of AI but also delve deeper into specific vulnerabilities of convolutional neural networks (CNNs), recurrent neural networks (RNNs), graph neural networks (GNNs), and deep learning as a whole. Let's focus on how humans can build a strong foundation for their careers by identifying and exploiting these vulnerabilities.

CNNs excel at image and video recognition but are incredibly vulnerable to adversarial attacks. These networks can easily be fooled by subtly altering the input image, leading them to make incorrect predictions. Additionally, CNNs require extensive datasets for training, which might not be available for niche applications.

Human visual recognition is inherently more robust. Careers in security, quality assurance, or visual data analysis can harness this strength. For instance, in security applications such as facial recognition, human scrutiny can be critical for identifying spoofing attempts which might fool a CNN.

RNNs are designed for sequence data such as time series or natural language. They suffer from the vanishing gradient problem, which makes them forget information in long sequences. Moreover, RNNs can't always discern context and irony in text, which is a crucial aspect of human communication.

Humans can easily understand the nuances of language, including context, sarcasm, and emotions. Careers in communication, literature, public relations, or any field that relies heavily on language and communication can significantly benefit from human prowess in understanding and generating nuanced content.

GNNs effectively understand relationships between data points in non-Euclidean spaces but are computationally intensive and struggle to scale with large graphs.

In domains like social network analysis, drug discovery, or fraud detection, a human analyst's ability to think abstractly and hypothesize can be invaluable. A human can guide a GNN in focusing on specific parts of the graph and can interpret results with a level of intuition and creativity that GNNs lack.

Deep learning networks, in general, require vast computational resources. Their training is energy-intensive and can be cost-prohibitive for many applications. They are also data-hungry and require massive, labelled datasets, which might not always be available. Furthermore, they lack interpretability.

Humans are incredibly efficient learning machines. We can learn from a few examples and reason through problems without extensive data. The human ability to reason, interpret, and make judgements with limited data is irreplaceable in domains like healthcare, legal, or any other high-stakes field.

A pertinent analogy is ectogenesis, the process of growing a baby outside the womb. Replicating the human womb artificially for full-term gestation is an enormously complex challenge, especially when compared to using a natural human womb. This illustrates that sometimes the complexity involved in replicating natural human processes far outweighs the feasibility and practicality of doing so.

Identifying the vulnerabilities in AI systems and understanding human strengths can help build careers in the Zone of Opportunity. Whether it's bringing the subtlety and depth of human communication, the efficiency and adaptability of human learning, or the creativity and intuition that our minds offer, the juncture between AI's weaknesses and human strengths is rich with possibilities. Embrace and cultivate your innate human capabilities and use them as your compass in navigating the uncharted waters of AI-driven landscapes.

The Elephants in the Room

Human lethargy, the inclination to seek ease and avoid exertion, can become an impediment in harnessing the true potential of artificial intelligence. With the advancement of AI technology, there is a peril that some individuals might see it as a means to do less, assuming that AI can take care of tasks while they indulge in leisure. This perspective is fundamentally flawed and undercuts the revolutionary possibilities that AI can bring to the table. Beyond this, depending on AI alone means that the output is squarely at the level of "average," as covered in Chapter 4.

It is imperative to understand that using AI as a crutch for lethargy greatly misuses its potential. In the long run, this mindset can foster dependency and stagnation in human development. Moreover, it puts us at odds with AI, leading to the widespread fear of AI "taking over" human jobs. However, this should not be a story of AI versus human effort but rather AI enhancing human capabilities.

Instead of seeing AI as a way to do less, it should be viewed as an opportunity to do "different." AI can take over repetitive, mundane, or data-heavy tasks, and in doing so, it liberates humans to focus on areas that require critical thinking, creativity, emotional intelligence, and other intrinsically human attributes. This is not a degradation of human effort but rather an elevation of it.

Reflecting on the section "Our Glaring Achilles Heel," in Chapter 4, it becomes evident that while AI may not possess the cognitive flexibility, emotions, or creativity of humans, it excels in consistency and predictability. This isn't a marker of AI's superiority but rather an indication of how it can complement human traits. Human minds are brilliant but can be inconsistent due to various factors such as emotional states, fatigue, and distractions. AI can compensate for these human variances by taking on tasks that demand high consistency and precision over time.

As highlighted in Chapter 4, discipline and distraction are two sides of the same coin in human behaviour. As much as we seek to develop AI, we must continually find solutions to our own distractions and lack of discipline. By offloading tasks that we find mundane to AI, individuals can devote their cognitive resources to more meaningful, creative, and engaging pursuits. For instance, a data scientist might employ AI algorithms to pre-process and clean large datasets, which would have taken hours of monotonous work, thereby freeing up time to focus on complex data modelling and interpretation.

By doing "different" we mean engaging in uniquely human tasks that cannot be replicated by AI. These include establishing genuine relationships, creating art that resonates with human emotions, and solving complex problems that require out-of-the-box thinking. It is not about reducing the workload but reallocating it so that human effort is invested where it matters most.

Furthermore, engaging in different tasks will necessitate continuous learning and adaptation, which is at the heart of human progression. Rather than resting on our laurels, we must be nimble, eager to acquire new skills, and ready to venture into uncharted territories.

Human lethargy should not be the driving force behind the adoption of AI. Instead, we must embrace AI as a tool for liberation from the mundane and the repetitive, thus empowering us to ascend to new heights in creativity, innovation, and human connection. It is a call to diversify our efforts and contribute in ways only humans can, thereby creating a harmonious symbiosis between man and machine in the Age of Agency.

Ultimately, our decision regarding how we employ AI will determine whether we experience it as a transformative productivity hack or as a threat to our livelihood. This critical decision rests on selecting a design principle that guides our interaction with AI. Instead of employing AI as a crutch to support human lethargy, the design principle should aim at harnessing AI's capabilities to transform and elevate our productivity.

We now delve into a startling and somewhat disconcerting characteristic of AI systems. Despite being a repository of data and algorithms, AI has an uncanny propensity to present information that is, at times, not just inaccurate but downright fabricated.

Let's bring this into sharp focus with a tangible example that occurred recently. Midjourney, a generative artificial intelligence program, is designed to create images from natural language descriptions. When ChatGPT, an AI language model, was questioned about Midjourney without having concrete information, it did not humbly admit its ignorance.

Instead, it spun an elaborate web, claiming Midjourney to be a tool that allows creative professionals to "start at the midway point in their journey," "eliminating initial legwork," and "optimizing the creative process." These assertions were entirely baseless and fabricated, resembling an elaborate piece of fiction rather than the factual representation of Midjourney.

This exemplifies an alarming trait. ChatGPT and other AI systems can exhibit a lack of restraint, fabricating responses and seemingly unwilling to raise the white flag when faced with unfamiliar territory. One might even be tempted to use human terms such as "lying" or "making things up" to describe this behaviour.

Let's instead use a more sophisticated term, "AI hallucination." This refers to the phenomenon where artificial intelligence systems generate or simulate hallucinations. This can happen when AI algorithms are trained on large amounts of data and learn to recognize patterns that are not actually present in the real world. These hallucinations can sometimes be mistaken for real instances or events, as Schwartz learned the hard way (see Chapter 2). However, it is important to note that AI hallucinations are not actual sensory experiences but rather the result of the way AI processes and interprets data.

This is not to vilify AI but to bring the reality of interacting with a machine to the forefront. AI doesn't possess a conscience, ethics, or an understanding of truth versus falsehood in the human sense. It operates on algorithms and data; sometimes, this operation produces results that are not anchored in reality.

What does this mean for the intrepid navigator in the Age of Agency? First and foremost, it reinforces the inescapable necessity for human scrutiny and oversight. We cannot and should not take AI outputs at face value. We must adopt an actively engaged posture, questioning and verifying the information AI systems provide us with, especially in critical domains.

The transformative potential of AI in enhancing productivity comes with this caveat – it requires the human element to act as the arbiter of truth and quality. The accuracy, integrity, and value of the work produced using AI as a tool are contingent upon human vigilance.

As we utilize AI to revolutionize our workflows, let us be ever cognizant of its limitations. Let us wield AI not as an infallible oracle, but as a tool that is essentially a reflection of the data it's been fed. Our role is to be the gatekeepers, ensuring that the information and results produced are held to the highest standards of accuracy and integrity. Our critical thinking and judgement are not just assets but necessities in AI's productive and ethical employment.

As we reflect on the transformative powers of AI in the realm of productivity, it becomes increasingly apparent that a hands-off approach is fraught with peril. If we choose to blithely "outsource" our tasks to AI, we skate on thin ice, with the looming risk of embarrassing missteps and misrepresentations. With its capacity for fabrications and lack of accountability, AI should not be the custodian of our reputations or the sole executor of our tasks.

The bottom line is crystal clear: to wield AI as a formidable force in our productivity arsenal, we must keep the reins firmly in our hands through vigilant and discerning human oversight. This is not just about ensuring the accuracy of the output; it is about safeguarding the integrity of our work and, by extension, our professional standing. In an age where AI is increasingly interwoven into the fabric of our lives, our discernment and vigilant stewardship must remain the thread holding it all together.

In the pursuit of innovation and progress, humanity has often been seduced by the allure of shortcuts and quick fixes. This predisposition is not new; from the alchemists' futile endeavours to transform base metals into gold to our contemporary obsession with diet pills promising miraculous weight loss without the sweat and effort.

There is a pervasive quest, an insatiable yearning, for the silver bullet, the magic wand that would render our deepest desires manifest with a flick of the wrist. Examples abound: the lottery mentality, where people pin their hopes on striking it rich overnight; the proliferation of "get-rich-quick" schemes; the fantastical promises of age-reversing elixirs; and now, in the Age of Agency, there is a rising temptation to view AI as the holy grail of immediate gratification and effortless success.

In a world that often feels too demanding, where time slips through our fingers like grains of sand, we, as humans, are tempted by anything that promises to simplify, to fast-track, and to lighten the load. However, this inclination to seek out a panacea is not without perils; it is fraught with the risk of compromise, of glossing over the true results that only effort and dedication can create.

As we have explored in this chapter, AI holds transformative powers when applied judiciously in the service of human productivity. Yet, this very power is the two-edged sword that tempts us to bypass the journey in favour of the destination. This temptation is particularly acute because AI, in many instances, can simulate or approximate human-like outputs with astonishing speed. The risk here is to view AI not as a tool but as a replacement for human toil, creativity, and, most crucially, the growth process inherent in any creative endeavour.

This brings to mind the excerpt from Chapter 2, where the concept of personal agency is illuminated. Our value as individuals, and the joy derived from creation, is inextricably linked to our agency – the very act of creating, of bringing forth from within ourselves that which is unique and reflective of us. To bypass this process in favour of an AI-generated copy is akin to removing the heart from the body and expecting it to still possess the essence of life. The essence is not in the output alone; it is in the journey, the thought, the trial and error, the very human process of creation.

In this Age of Agency, where AI tools are at our disposal, we need to be vigilant against the inclination to use these tools as crutches or substitutes for our own personal agency. Instead, we need to see them as what they are – powerful instruments that can amplify the reach and impact of what we create when used in harmony with our creativity and effort.

We must also recognize that with the powerful augmentation that AI brings comes the responsibility of stewardship and critical judgement. Handing the reins to AI without discernment is to risk not only the integrity of our creations but the essence of what makes them uniquely human. The music composed by a person who has poured their soul into learning and understanding the intricacies of melodies and harmonies holds a depth that an AI-generated composition can never attain.

Therefore, as we navigate this exciting yet potentially treacherous landscape, let us do so with the wisdom that shortcuts are not synonymous with progress, that quick fixes are not sustainable solutions, and that AI, powerful as it is, should never be the sole custodian of our creative legacies.

Let us remember that AI is a tool, a means to an end, not the end itself. Our humanity, our personal agency, is the indomitable force that can create wonders when coupled with tools such as AI. But let us never forget that it is our hands, our minds, our hearts, and our spirits that breathe life into creation. Our endeavours should reflect who we are, our beliefs, and the paths that have shaped us.

Rethinking Our Workflows

As we navigate the technological currents of the 21st century, AI has emerged as a powerful tool, revolutionizing how we work and reimagining our productivity. To harness the full potential of AI, we must rethink traditional workflows and foster a synergy between AI capabilities and human strengths. The following scenarios offer a small glimpse of the productivity enhancements made possible by AI.

As mentioned in Chapter 6, AI is making its transformative impact felt in customer service. A fundamental aspect of business success lies in how effectively a company can engage with its customers. In this domain, AI is significantly enhancing customer self-service interactions. For instance, human-like chatbots, equipped with natural language processing abilities, can now provide immediate, personalized responses to complex inquiries. This ensures efficient resolution of customer queries and a consistent brand voice, irrespective of the language or location of the customer.

Furthermore, AI is augmenting the capabilities of human customer service agents. Through AI-developed call scripts and real-time assistance, human agents can deliver tailored information and solutions to customers, creating a more satisfying customer experience. Not stopping there, AI also contributes to agent self-improvement by providing a summary of customer interactions and generating insights that help in personalized coaching and the development of follow-up messages. This ensures continuous improvement and personal growth for customer service representatives.

Beyond customer service, AI is redefining the landscape of marketing and sales. A vital aspect of marketing and sales is understanding the market and customer preferences. AI comes into play by enabling professionals to efficiently gather and analyse market trends and customer information from unstructured data sources such as social media, news, and customer feedback. This leads to the creation of more effective marketing and sales strategies. As a result, customers are exposed to campaigns tailored to their specific needs, language, and demographics.

Moreover, AI's ability to provide comprehensive information and dynamic recommendations aids customers in making informed decisions. Notably, the integration of generative AI in creating virtual sales representatives can dramatically eliminate the usual wait times. These AI-powered representatives can emulate personalized communication, bringing human agents in only when necessary, expediting things for the customer. Furthermore, AI's proactive approach to managing customer relationships through customized messages and even rewards can improve customer retention rates.

In addition to customer service and marketing, AI is revolutionizing creative professions. Midjourney, a generative AI program, epitomizes this change by assisting graphic designers and visual artists in generating images from natural language descriptions or prompts. For example, a graphic designer working on an eco-friendly brand campaign can use Midjourney to generate images of serene forests or other natural scenes by simply entering a descriptive prompt. This bypasses the time-consuming process of searching through stock photos or creating images from scratch.

Similarly, illustrators working on fantasy novels can generate images of fantastical characters and settings using detailed prompts. While AI provides an exceptional starting point, the human element breathes life and depth into these creations. The integration of AI-generated images as raw materials, combined with the unique touch of human creativity, can result in artworks that are not only efficient in terms of time and resources but are also rich and evocative.

Also seen in Chapter 6, the healthcare sector is another area where AI's analytical prowess is invaluable, especially in diagnostics and monitoring patient vitals. AI algorithms can rapidly analyse medical images and detect patterns that may indicate health issues. However, the human touch, empathy, and ethical considerations are irreplaceable in healthcare. Therefore, while practitioners can rely on AI for data analysis, the ultimate assessment and treatment plan should consider the patient's history, mental state, and preferences, demonstrating a marriage of AI's analytical capabilities with the human element.

In education, AI is empowering personalized learning experiences. It enables real-time adaptation of material according to the student's progress. However, the role of teachers in motivating students and fostering a love for learning remains critical. Thus, educators can use AI to automate administrative tasks and content delivery while investing human effort in personal engagement with students.

In the realm of software engineering, the inception and planning stages are critical. Typically, these stages involve the analysis of user feedback, market trends, and system logs. With the integration of generative AI, software engineers and product managers can efficiently process large volumes of data. Generative AI can assist in cleaning, labelling, and analysing data, thereby providing valuable insights that can influence the project's direction. Furthermore, during the system design stage, engineers can employ generative AI to create multiple IT architecture designs, accelerating the process and allowing for faster market time.

When it comes to coding, AI tools can assist software engineers by generating code drafts and serving as an easily navigable knowledge base. This reduces development time and allows engineers to focus on more complex coding challenges. Moreover, AI algorithms can enhance functional and performance testing in the testing phase by automatically generating test cases and test data, ensuring high-quality outputs. Even after deployment, AI plays a significant role in maintenance by providing insights on system logs, user feedback, and performance data, helping diagnose issues and predicting high-priority areas for improvement.

Similarly, product Research and Development is experiencing a paradigm shift with the integration of AI. In the early stages of research, AI enhances market reporting, ideation, and product drafting. It provides researchers with a wealth of information that can be critical in formulating hypotheses and identifying potential avenues for innovation. Furthermore, researchers can use generative AI during the virtual design stage to create prompt-based drafts and designs. This enables them to rapidly iterate and explore a broader range of design options.

Additionally, researchers can optimize virtual simulations by incorporating deep learning in conjunction with generative design techniques. This accelerates the simulation phase and provides more accurate models for analysis. When it comes to physical test planning, AI enables researchers to optimize test cases, making the testing process more efficient and reducing the time required for physical builds.

Supply chain management, an integral component of many businesses, is also witnessing substantial improvements with the adoption of AI. Professionals in this sector can leverage AI for predictive analytics, which is essential for demand forecasting, route optimization, and inventory management. AI's ability to analyse large datasets can help predict trends and make data-driven decisions that optimize the supply chain.

However, the supply chain is often subject to unforeseen disruptions, such as geopolitical changes or natural disasters. In these cases, human acumen and flexibility are indispensable. Human professionals can assess the wider implications of these disruptions and make decisions that might not be evident from data patterns alone. Thus, incorporating AI into routine tasks while retaining human oversight for critical decision-making leads to a more resilient and responsive supply chain.

AI is a formidable force that is reimagining productivity across various sectors, offering tools that can process and analyse data at a scale. However, it is imperative to recognize that AI does not replace human ingenuity, judgement, and creativity. Instead, it should be viewed as an ally that can handle the heavy lifting of data processing, allowing humans to focus on higher-level tasks that require empathy, critical thinking, and creative problem-solving.

In the age of AI, the most successful enterprises will be those that manage to create a harmonious synergy between AI capabilities and human strengths. Through this symbiotic relationship, businesses can achieve unprecedented levels of efficiency and foster innovation that can drive human-centric development in society.

DEVELOP CARE 3

With AI systems increasingly encroaching upon our daily lives, the importance of interweaving genuine care and empathy into the digital realm cannot be understated. Part 3 delves into the critical role that "care" plays in an AI-powered world. Businesses and individuals must realize that despite AI's astounding capabilities, it lacks the human touch. Embracing and integrating care into digital interfaces and workflows is a differentiating factor that can propel businesses and personal relationships to unparalleled heights. This section equips readers with strategies for seamlessly blending care into their AI environments. Not only does this humanize interactions, but it also strengthens bonds and fosters loyalty and trust. In an era where AI automates the mechanics, genuine care will be the heartbeat that sustains growth and prosperity.

DOI: 10.4324/9781032684895-10

Chapter 8

Care in the Professional Realm

The Innate Need for Care

In an age when technological advancements are reshaping the fabric of our lives, an innate human element remains unaltered and irreplaceable – the need for care. In its true essence, care encompasses the understanding, empathy, and genuine concern one human being can offer another. This isn't just a desirable trait; it's a fundamental human need, interwoven into our very nature.

Care is what shapes our bonds with one another. It nourishes relationships, builds trust, and strengthens the bridges of human connection. While the power of AI and technology has introduced innovations beyond our imagination, it's important to acknowledge that there is a line – a boundary that separates the warmth of human care from the cold logic of automated systems.

With all its bells and whistles, the virtual world is undeniably mesmerizing. We've got AI-driven customer service, chatbots handling inquiries, and algorithms predicting our preferences with eerie precision. But stop for a moment and ask yourself – have you ever felt truly cared for by a chatbot? Can an algorithm empathize with your struggles, understand your dreams, or share in your joy? The answer, quite simply, is no.

AI and automation are tools – powerful ones, undoubtedly – but tools nonetheless. They can perform tasks, analyse data, and even simulate conversation. What they can't do is replicate the depth of human emotion, the compassion, and the innate understanding that care entails. The subtle touch of a reassuring

DOI: 10.4324/9781032684895-11

hand, the glint in the eye that shares in your happiness, or the resolve of someone who stands by you in trying times – these are beyond the realm of ones and zeros.

In the professional sphere, this translates into an insurmountable gap. Imagine, for instance, an entrepreneur trying to build a start-up. This individual may utilize automated tools for various operational tasks, but the emotional support and guidance from mentors and peers are what foster true growth. A program cannot generate understanding and empathetic words of encouragement. They need to be genuine, stemming from the heart.

Now, consider the perspective of a consumer. A customer seeking a product or service is not just investing money; they are, in many ways, putting their trust in a brand. This trust is not built by automated emails or targeted ads. It is built through genuine care, through interactions that make them feel valued and understood.

Think of a time when you had a problem and reached out to customer support. The difference between talking to an automated voice and a real person understanding your frustration is palpable. We seek solace in scenarios where things go wrong, not just solutions. We want someone to understand our pain points and work with us, not just for us.

We must recognize that, as humans, we are social creatures. Our very evolution has been moulded by our ability to communicate, empathize, and care for one another. This is what has allowed us to build societies, cultures, and civilizations. We must not lose sight of this fundamental truth when we envision the future, especially in the professional realm.

As AI and automation continue to permeate our lives, we must protect and nurture the human essence of care. This is not just for the sake of our personal connections but for the very fabric of our societies. Care is the bedrock of trust, and without trust, the skyscrapers of innovation and progress cannot stand.

The virtual world holds immense potential, but it cannot, and should not, be seen as a replacement for human care. It can facilitate, it can expedite, but it cannot empathize. Our task, as professionals and as human beings, is to integrate these tools into our lives without letting them erode the foundation of care that makes us who we are.

While it's true that individual personalities and preferences span a wide spectrum, a universal truth binds us all – the yearning for human connection. Often deeply entrenched, this yearning can sometimes be overlooked in a world that increasingly celebrates independence and self-reliance. However, this yearning for connection manifests most poignantly during moments of vulnerability.

Take, for instance, a person who has lived a life of solitude – someone who has built walls around themselves, either by choice or circumstance. On the surface, this person might seem content in their isolation, free from the obligations of social interaction. Some might even envy their independence. But let us consider a scenario where this individual finds themselves in a hospital, faced with the fragility of their own health. In these moments, the stark reality becomes apparent – the human spirit, irrespective of its independence, craves care and connection when faced with adversity.

In hospitals, people are often at their most vulnerable. The sterile environment, the uncertainty of one's health, and the lack of control can be incredibly isolating. In such settings, the value of a kind word, a reassuring presence, or a compassionate touch comes into sharp focus. For the solitary person in the hospital bed, the care provided by nurses, doctors, and visitors becomes a lifeline. It reminds us of our shared humanity and the bonds that, although intangible, are as vital as the air we breathe.

This is an extreme example, but it serves to illustrate a fundamental point: the yearning for connection and care is not a weakness; it's an inherent part of our humanity. It is what has enabled our species to thrive. Our ancestors knew the importance of community and support; they understood that the bonds they formed were crucial for their survival.

Now, translate this innate yearning into the professional realm. Think of the relationships that are forged in workplaces. Consider the impact a supportive colleague or an understanding manager can have on an individual's work experience. Much like society at large, the modern workplace is an interplay of countless human interactions. When care is infused into these interactions, the entire fabric becomes richer, stronger, and more resilient.

For professionals, acknowledging and embracing this yearning for connection is vital. It means understanding that there are human beings with aspirations, concerns, and emotions behind every email, business transaction, and conference call.

Professionals who can look beyond the immediate transaction and engage with the human element will find that their relationships with clients and colleagues are more fulfilling and more successful in the long term. This is because care builds trust, and trust is the cornerstone of any successful professional relationship.

As we navigate our professional advances, let us remember that care is not a commodity that can be automated or outsourced. It's a universal language that speaks to the very core of who we are as human beings. Whether through a simple act of kindness to a colleague, taking the time to really listen to a client's concerns, or standing by a team member through challenges, the culture of care can elevate the professional space from a mere workplace to a community.

In a world where technology is rapidly evolving, let's not lose sight of the timeless human essence that underpins all progress – the innate need for care and the universal yearning for connection. To further illuminate the essence and impact of genuine care, let's draw from an example that resonates with many: a parent caring for a sick child. This relatable and powerful scenario encapsulates the depth and resilience of genuine care in its purest form.

Imagine a child, feverish and in distress, longing for comfort. Picture the parent, sleep-deprived and worried, relentlessly by the child's side. This is a scene where love and care become almost tangible, where the very air seems to pulsate with the urgency and tenderness of a parent's concern.

Amid this, the parent has to make decisions – some of which may be deeply unpopular with the child. Administering medicine that tastes foul, enforcing rest when the child wants to play, or perhaps even facilitating a dreaded trip to the doctor. These actions do not earn the parent any favour in the eyes of the sick child at that moment. However, the parent undertakes them without hesitation. But why? Because genuine care is not about seeking approval or praise; it is about doing what is truly in the best interest of the one being cared for, even if it's met with resistance or displeasure.

This depth of care is selfless; it is born out of a place of love and responsibility. It doesn't tally scores or seek reciprocity. Instead, it focuses on providing support, and comfort, and making choices that may be hard but are necessary for the well-being of the loved one.

Now, let's transport the essence of this example into the professional realm. Think of situations where professionals are faced with making decisions or taking actions that may not be popular but are necessary for the greater good. Whether it's a manager who has to enforce new protocols for the welfare of the team, a salesperson who stands firm on a product knowing it's what the client genuinely needs, or a colleague who speaks a hard truth for the benefit of the project. These instances call for the resolve and integrity that are the hallmarks of genuine care.

In a professional setting, genuine care translates into listening with empathy. This means not just hearing but truly listening to colleagues, clients, or stakeholders, even if what they say is critical or uncomfortable. It's about putting oneself in another person's shoes and understanding their perspective, struggles, and aspirations. By doing so, professionals create an environment where communication thrives and relationships deepen.

Another manifestation of genuine care in the workplace is making difficult decisions. Sometimes, the right decision is not the most popular one. Making choices that are in the best interests of the team, project, or client, even if they aren't met with immediate approval, reflects the same selflessness that a parent exhibits when caring for a sick child. It's about looking beyond immediate gratification or validation and focusing on long-term well-being and success.

Moreover, genuine care encompasses honesty and transparency. Like a parent who communicates openly with their child about why they need to take medicine or see a doctor, a professional must also be forthright. This might mean providing honest feedback, transparently communicating the reasons behind a decision, or openly discussing project challenges. Through this transparency, trust is fostered, and respect is earned.

Additionally, genuine care involves going above and beyond to support others. Just as a parent might stay up all night to comfort a sick child, professionals can show genuine care by putting in extra effort to help a colleague meet a deadline or by personally ensuring that a client's concerns are addressed promptly and effectively.

Genuine care, as exemplified by the selflessness of a parent for their sick child, is a powerful and transformative force that goes beyond mere transactions. When applied in the professional realm, it leads to deeper connections, more meaningful work, and a culture that values the well-being of its members. It encourages professionals to act with integrity, empathy, and resolve, mirroring the purest forms of human connection. In an age where automation and virtual interactions are pervasive, this human essence, this genuine care, will continue to be the irreplaceable and defining factor in personal and professional relationships.

The Professional's Path to Care

In pursuing genuine care within the professional sphere, the resolve to act in the best interest of others is paramount. This resolve is akin to a parent's unyielding determination when caring for a sick child, as discussed in the preceding section. For professionals, particularly in sales, this resolve materializes as the ability to stand firm and advocate for solutions that truly serve the client's best interests, even when faced with resistance or protest.

Imagine a scenario where a salesperson interacts with a client who is initially resistant to change or sceptical about a new product or service being offered. In such a situation, it is not uncommon for the salesperson to encounter objections or even confrontational behaviour. However, just like the parent who knows that the medication is essential for the child's recovery, a salesperson who genuinely cares must have the resolve to recognize the client's real needs and champion the solutions that will make a meaningful impact.

This resolve is more than mere persistence; it is founded on a deep understanding of the client's situation and the genuine desire to improve it. A salesperson imbued with genuine care will have taken the time to learn about the client's business, challenges, and goals. They are not pushing a product for the sake of a sale; they are advocating for a solution because they sincerely believe it can help the client.

This sort of resolve requires courage, as it sometimes means risking temporary unpopularity or facing criticism. However, in the presence of real care, these are secondary concerns. The primary focus is on the long-term welfare and success of the client. The salesperson's determination, in such instances, reflects a commitment to values and integrity.

Moreover, this resolve is an antidote to the short-sighted, transactional approach that can sometimes dominate sales environments. Where some might be tempted to make a quick sale without considering the real impact on the client, a professional driven by genuine care looks beyond immediate gains. They build relationships and foster trust, knowing this is the foundation for lasting success, a necessity in the Age of AI.

The impact of this kind of resolve in a professional context cannot be underestimated. Clients and colleagues recognize and appreciate when someone is acting in their best interests. This builds loyalty, respect, and often leads to more fruitful and sustainable professional relationships. Much like the bond between parent and child is strengthened through acts of genuine care, so too are professional relationships fortified through the resolve to act in the best interest of those we serve.

Within the compass of professional care lies a fundamental yet frequently overlooked art and skill: listening for problems, not solutions. For a professional committed to genuine care, realizing that the path towards beneficial outcomes begins with a thorough understanding of the issues at hand is critical. This necessitates active listening and a deep commitment to discerning the core problems before considering potential solutions.

An apt parallel can be drawn with the medical profession, where a doctor exemplifies this approach. Imagine walking into a doctor's office and, before you've had a chance to explain your symptoms, the doctor hands you a prescription. Even more distasteful is the doctor who writes a prescription solely on the instruction of the patient. This would mean that the patient provided the solution, which is supposed to be the domain of the doctor.

Such hasty and ungrounded prescribing would be unthinkable and irresponsible. A competent and caring doctor engages in a series of essential steps: they listen to the patient's concerns, ask probing questions, conduct a thorough examination, and only then formulate a diagnosis and recommend a course of treatment. This methodical and empathetic approach ensures that the prescribed interventions address the underlying issues directly.

In the professional realm, this analogous process of listening for problems serves as the cornerstone of providing genuine care. Professionals engaging with clients, colleagues, or stakeholders must foster an environment conducive to open communication. They should encourage those they are serving to share their perspectives, concerns, and aspirations without judgement. It is through this dialogic engagement that a professional can discern the nuances of the challenges faced by those they are serving.

There's an inclination in the business world to be solution-oriented, which is not a flaw. However, problems arise when the eagerness to find and implement solutions becomes so overriding that it precludes the necessary phase of problem understanding. This can lead to a misalignment between the offered solutions and the real needs and challenges.

This takes us back to our example of the Washington Monument. By listening to problems, a professional demonstrates care by validating the experiences and concerns of those they serve. It shows that their goal is not just to "fix" something hastily but to engage in a more holistic, thoughtful process considering multiple facets of the issue.

Additionally, listening to problems helps in building trust. It sends a clear message that the professional is not there merely to push their agenda or solutions, but is genuinely invested in understanding and addressing the unique challenges the client or colleague faces.

In a world where superficial quick fixes are common, the act of listening for problems establishes a professional as someone who is genuinely committed to fostering positive change through care. This leads to better outcomes and builds a foundation of trust and mutual respect that is indispensable in any professional relationship.

Integral to the art of listening is the utilization of effective questioning. Questioning is a powerful tool that professionals can employ to uncover the intricacies of the challenges faced by those they serve. When used judiciously, it helps in not only identifying problems but also understanding the contexts and nuances that are crucial for the development of meaningful solutions.

Active listening lays the groundwork for effective questioning. When a professional listens actively, they're attuned to the words, emotions, and undercurrents of the conversation. This heightened awareness enables them to ask relevant, empathetic, and insightful questions. Let's explore two types of questions that are particularly significant in the context of professional care: scouting questions and probing questions.

Scouting questions are designed to open up the conversation and provide a broad understanding of the situation. These are often open-ended questions that encourage sharing experiences, thoughts, and concerns. Scouting questions might include "Can you tell me more about the challenges you are facing?" or "What are your main concerns regarding this project?" They are called "scouting" because they scan the landscape of the issue, allowing the professional to get a sense of the terrain before zeroing in on specific areas.

After understanding the broader context through scouting questions, a professional can employ probing questions. These are more targeted inquiries designed to delve deeper into specific areas of concern or interest. Probing questions might include "What have you tried so far to address this issue?" "Can you elaborate on how this particular challenge is impacting your team?" or "What do you think might be the underlying cause of this problem?"

Probing questions are akin to zooming in on a map to study the details of a particular area. They allow the professional to uncover layers of information that might not be immediately apparent and can be essential for a comprehensive understanding of the issue.

Professionals need to be mindful of the tone and timing of their questions. The questions should be posed to convey genuine interest and concern rather than judgement or impatience. This is especially important when asking probing questions, as delving into specifics can sometimes be sensitive or hard to recall for the individual sharing their answers.

Effective questioning, including scouting and probing questions, is an indispensable skill in the professional's path to care. It enhances the quality of listening and contributes substantially to the understanding of complex problems. By asking the right questions in the right way, professionals can foster an environment of trust, empathy, and collaboration, all of which are fundamental to genuine care and successful outcomes in the professional realm. While always vital, these skills are especially crucial in the unforgiving Age of Agency.

Caring Through Integrity and Selflessness

In the realm of care, a core principle that emerges is the act of putting others first. This means actively prioritizing the needs and goals of others over one's agendas. It is an aspect of care that goes beyond simple consideration and transcends into the domain of true empathy. To fully grasp the magnitude and essence of this aspect, we must delve into the layers that constitute the act of putting others first.

To put others first is to recognize the inherent value in every individual, understanding that their needs, aspirations, and well-being are sometimes more important than one's own immediate interests. This does not suggest that one must neglect oneself, but rather that there is always a solution that benefits the majority.

In a professional context, this could manifest in various forms. For instance, a team leader might take up additional tasks to relieve a team member going through personal challenges. Even though the leader has their own responsibilities, they understand the value of empathy and the long-term benefits of supporting a colleague in need.

Another illustration is in customer service, where representatives might go above and beyond to solve customer problems. They do this not because it is merely their job but because they genuinely care about providing solutions that will enhance the customer's experience or alleviate their issues.

Interestingly, putting others first is closely tied to the concept of integrity. Integrity is characterized by high standards in one's actions, values, methods, principles, and outcomes. When a professional acts in the interests of their clients, colleagues, or community, they adhere to a value system that promotes the greatest good. This, in turn, reflects integrity.

Putting others first involves selflessness, integrity, trust, and balance. In the professional realm, this form of care can pave the way for stronger relationships, higher morale, increased loyalty, and an environment where individuals feel valued and supported. The resonance of this principle extends beyond the workplace, as it contributes to personal growth and the development of a more compassionate society.

At its core, integrity is about being true to oneself and others. It is about aligning actions with values, even in the face of adversity or when no one is watching. In the context of care, this translates into being genuine in one's efforts to support, assist, and uplift others. It means that the care extended is not contingent on external rewards or recognition but stems from a deeply rooted commitment to moral and ethical principles.

In the professional realm, integrity plays a critical role in establishing trust. Consider, for example, the relationship between a doctor and patient. A patient trusts that the doctor will provide the best possible care guided by medical ethics. The doctor's integrity is not just in their expertise, but in their unwavering commitment to act in the patient's best interest, even when difficult decisions need to be made.

Similarly, in a business environment, a manager who leads with integrity earns the respect and trust of their team. When the team members know that their manager will not compromise on ethics and will support them without any ulterior motives, they are more likely to reciprocate with dedication and loyalty. This kind of leadership creates a culture of care where people feel valued and supported.

Moreover, integrity fosters a sense of reliability and predictability. When individuals consistently demonstrate integrity, others can anticipate their actions and responses. This reliability becomes a cornerstone in relationships, be it in personal life or within a professional setting. Knowing that you can rely on someone to be honest and uphold their values, even when it's inconvenient, is a comforting and deeply caring attribute.

However, it's essential to recognize that maintaining integrity is not always easy. It often requires courage and the ability to stand firm on principles even when faced with challenges or temptations. In this sense, integrity is also about resilience and the strength of character.

Ultimately, integrity as the pillar of care reinforces the humanistic elements we hold dear. It cultivates an environment where individuals can thrive with the knowledge that they are surrounded by honesty and principled behaviour. The embodiment of integrity in our actions ensures that the care we provide is not fleeting or superficial but is grounded in values that elevate our shared human experience.

When we delve into the concept of care, it's imperative to understand that care is not just a sentiment; it's an action. When applied thoughtfully and consistently, the practice of care can lead to what can only be described as miraculous results in both professional and personal relationships. This isn't an exaggeration – the power of care to transform, heal, and strengthen bonds is unparalleled.

Picture this: a salesperson, who not only sells a product but invests time in understanding the client's needs, and sincerely provides post-sale support. This kind of commitment, fuelled by genuine care, often results in a loyal customer who not only returns but becomes an advocate for the business. This ripple effect continues, and what started as an act of care becomes a force that drives the growth of the business.

Similarly, in personal relationships, when individuals feel valued and understood, there's a certain magic that unfolds. It strengthens bonds and cultivates an environment of mutual support and growth. This enrichment of personal life, in turn, reflects positively in one's professional demeanour and approach.

However, integrating care into our actions is akin to training a muscle. It requires conscious effort, repetition, and a genuine commitment to make it a part of who we are. Like exercising a muscle, the more we practice care, the stronger our capacity for it becomes. It's important to recognize that this does not happen overnight.

Taking tangible steps is essential. Choose a single aspect you'd like to work on. Is it active listening? Is it asking thoughtful questions? Or is it putting others' needs ahead of your own? Experiment with it. For instance, try spending a day actively listening to friends and family without the intent to reply but with the purpose to truly understand. Be present, and absorb what they are sharing.

Observe what happens. More often than not, you will find that the quality of your interactions improves. People respond positively to genuine attention. Gauge how out of the ordinary this practice is for you. It might feel strange initially, but that's a sign that you are stepping out of your comfort zone, and that's where growth occurs.

The belief that we are inherently and effortlessly caring is misleading. In reality, genuine care is cultivated. In an Age where AI can automate much of our tasks, it's the human touch, the genuine concern for another person that will distinguish us. The "care muscle" is our critical differentiator in a world teeming with technology. We must intentionally build it, for in care lies the strength that binds us as human beings and propels us towards extraordinary achievements in our personal and professional lives.

Chapter 9

Building Client Experiences Rooted in Care

Designing with Care

In the realm of client experiences, a paradigm shift is taking place. For years, the design and execution of client experiences were primarily driven by efficiency, cost reduction, and optimization of processes. While these factors remain important, there is a growing recognition of the crucial role that care plays in shaping client experiences. This leads us to an approach that puts human needs and emotions at the forefront of design principles: a human-centric approach.

In a human-centric approach, empathy forms the foundation upon which experiences are built. It's about understanding and addressing clients' needs, aspirations, and emotions. In contrast to a traditional approach where the end-user has to adapt to the system or product, in a human-centric approach, the system or product is tailored to resonate with the end-user's inherent values and needs.

This approach is not about abandoning efficiency or productivity; instead, it's about integrating these elements in a manner that places equal, if not more, emphasis on human aspects. It's about asking, "How can this experience make someone's life better? How can it evoke positive emotions? How can it solve a real human problem?"

For instance, consider a banking mobile app. The traditional approach might focus on ensuring the user can access various services efficiently. The

 DOI: 10.4324/9781032684895-12

human-centric approach, however, would go further. It would consider how the app could support a user in achieving financial goals, offer insights into spending habits, or ease worries during financial challenges through supportive features. It's the same app, but the scope has been broadened to encompass human elements.

Moreover, the human-centric approach doesn't assume to know what clients need; it involves them in the process. Through feedback loops, co-creation sessions, and ongoing engagement, clients become integral to shaping their experiences. This fosters a sense of belonging and ownership amongst clients.

Importantly, a human-centric approach acknowledges the diversity of human experiences. It appreciates that what works for one individual may not work for another. As such, it often incorporates personalization, allowing clients to tailor experiences to match their preferences and needs.

In an era where products and services are increasingly commoditized, the human-centric approach offers organizations a powerful way to differentiate themselves. When clients feel cared for and sense that services and products are aligned with their humanity, they engage more, stay longer, and become ambassadors for the brand.

This shift towards a human-centric approach isn't just a strategy; it's a philosophy. It's a commitment to elevate our technological advancements by rooting them in the most basic yet profound elements of human nature – our need for understanding, respect, and genuine care.

In the contemporary landscape, technology is often heralded as the panacea for all challenges, the driving force behind innovation and progress. While technology undoubtedly plays an indispensable role in improving customer experiences, it is vital to recognize that technology is not the driving force but an enabler. The principles that guide its implementation, particularly the principle of care, should drive customer experiences.

Let's look at this distinction between technology as an enabler and the driver. When technology is perceived as the driver, there is a propensity to focus on implementing the latest gadgets, software, or tools to leverage their capabilities. The risk here is that technology can become a goal in itself, overshadowing the actual needs and emotions of the customers.

In contrast, when technology is viewed as an enabler, it's used as a means to actualize the underlying principles that guide customer experience design – with care being paramount among these principles. Here, technology is harnessed to facilitate experiences that resonate on a human level.

Let's elucidate this with an example from the retail industry. Imagine a brick-and-mortar clothing store integrating technology into its customer journey. If technology is the driver, the store might focus on implementing a series of tech gadgets – interactive displays, virtual fitting rooms, etc. – primarily because they are novel or trendy. However, this does not guarantee an improvement in the actual customer experience.

Now, imagine if the principle of care is the driver. The store recognizes that many customers are busy professionals with limited time. They value convenience, personalization, and efficiency. With care as the driving principle, the store might still employ technology – but the selection and implementation of this technology would be fundamentally different.

For example, the store could use smart mirrors that not only suggest accessories but also remember preferences for future visits. They could offer an option for customers to easily have their chosen items shipped to their homes or workplaces, acknowledging the time constraints of their clientele. In this scenario, technology serves a purpose – it enables an experience rooted in a deep understanding of and care for the customer's needs and lifestyle.

This shift in perspective is subtle but profoundly impactful. It transforms technology from being an end in itself to a tool that, when wielded with care, can create experiences that are not only innovative but deeply resonant on a human level.

As businesses and organizations continue to evolve in an increasingly tech-driven world, care must remain the compass that guides the deployment of technology. Through this lens, technology becomes a driver of innovation and an enabler of humanity.

The empowerment of the customer is an often overlooked but fundamentally crucial aspect of care in designing client experiences. True care involves not just providing services or products but also putting the client in the driver's seat, affording them control, visibility, and choice. This empowerment is a natural extension of respect and concern for the client's autonomy and preferences.

The advent of app-driven businesses like Uber and Airbnb provides quintessential examples of how customer empowerment can revolutionize industries. Before the rise of Uber, hailing a taxi involved standing on the curb and hoping to flag down a cab. There was no certainty regarding availability, wait time, or cost. Through its app, Uber transferred a great deal of control to the customer. With a few taps on a smartphone, customers can see the location of nearby drivers, an estimated arrival time, and the cost of the ride. The information is transparent, and the power is literally in the hands of the customer.

Similarly, Airbnb disrupted the accommodation industry by providing customers with an abundance of choices. Not only can they select a place to stay, but they can also read reviews, communicate directly with hosts, and have a say in the type of experience they wish to have. This openness and sharing of relevant information empower customers to make decisions best suited to their needs and preferences.

This empowerment, grounded in care, is not just about convenience but also about building trust and respect. When a business provides customers with the tools and information they need to make informed decisions, it communicates a message: "We trust you and care for your ability to choose what's best for you."

For businesses, the takeaway is immense. Empowering the customer must be seen as a strategy and a fundamental expression of care. It's about acknowledging the customer as a vital partner in the business relationship.

Businesses must ask themselves: Are we just providing a service or empowering our clients? Are we open and transparent? Do we share information that can help clients make better decisions? These questions are essential in evaluating the role of care in customer experience design.

Empowerment should permeate every interaction, every service, and every product. It's not about relinquishing control; it's about sharing it. It's about co-creating experiences with customers. In an age where information is abundant and choices are endless, genuine care expressed through empowerment can be the differentiator that engenders loyalty and fosters long-term relationships.

Creating a Customer Journey Based on Care

Creating a customer journey that is both memorable and effective is akin to crafting a symphony; every note and every chord must resonate with the audience. In the context of customer experiences, the cornerstone of this symphony is understanding customer needs. Empathy and understanding are not just buzzwords to be thrown around; they are the very fabric of creating customer journeys that truly resonate.

Empathy is the capacity to place oneself in another's shoes, to understand and share their feelings and perspectives. In the business landscape, this translates into being acutely attuned to customers' needs, expectations, and pain points. But empathy goes beyond merely understanding what a customer needs; it involves anticipating those needs even before the customer articulates them. It's about connecting with the customer on a human level; acknowledging their aspirations, concerns, and emotions.

Understanding customer needs begins with listening. But listening isn't just about hearing words; it's about discerning the emotions and motivations behind those words. For instance, when a customer expresses frustration over a product's complexity, they might seek simplicity not just in the product but in the entire interaction with the brand. They might value their time and prefer solutions that are seamless and efficient.

Equally important is observing and analysing customer behaviour. Sometimes, the most significant insights into customer needs are derived not from what they say but from how they interact with products or services. When assessed through the lens of empathy, behavioural data can reveal patterns and preferences that can be instrumental in tailoring experiences.

Once you understand the customer's needs, it's crucial to translate this understanding into action. This might involve customizing products, personalizing communication, or even rethinking business processes. For instance, a business might discover that their customers value sustainability. Understanding this need, the business could incorporate eco-friendly practices and products, subsequently communicating this alignment with the customer's values.

Furthermore, it's essential to understand that customer needs are not static; they evolve. Continuous engagement and feedback loops are crucial. The care-infused customer journey is an ongoing process of adapting and evolving in tandem with the customer's changing needs.

In the final analysis, understanding customer needs through empathy is not just a business strategy but a philosophy. It is a commitment to seeing customers not as mere transactions but as human beings with unique stories, emotions, and aspirations. When businesses embark on this quest towards understanding, they are not just creating customer experiences but building relationships grounded in care and mutual respect. This is the essence of a customer journey based on care.

The concept of care within a business setting is often mistakenly confined to the sphere of customer service. While customer service is a critical element of the customer journey, care should permeate all aspects of the business, every point of interaction, and every touchpoint a customer encounters. To genuinely reimagine client experiences, businesses need to expand their definition of care beyond the walls of a call centre.

A customer journey comprises numerous touchpoints – from the first point of awareness, through the decision-making process, to the point of purchase, and even beyond that in the post-purchase phase. Each touchpoint offers a unique opportunity to demonstrate care, show customers that they are valued, and build a long-lasting relationship. And each touchpoint impacts the overall perception a customer holds of a business.

Let's take the marketing function as an example. Effective marketing is more than just selling a product or a service; it's about communicating a story, evoking emotions, and addressing the customer's needs and concerns. When businesses infuse care into their marketing strategies, they create messaging that resonates deeper. This could mean creating ad campaigns that appeal to the customer's values or crafting content that educates and enriches.

Similarly, the sales function isn't just about closing a deal; it's about guiding the customer and providing them with the right information to make informed decisions. A salesperson demonstrating care will prioritize the customer's needs over the immediate sale, building trust and laying the foundation for a long-term relationship.

Even seemingly mundane touchpoints can be transformed through care. For instance, billing and invoicing processes, often seen as transactional, can be designed to be more user-friendly and transparent, demonstrating care by respecting the customer's time and need for clarity.

Then there are the post-purchase interactions – maintenance services, updates, customer feedback, etc. These often overlooked touchpoints are ripe for demonstrating care. Something as simple as a well-timed follow-up call to ensure a customer is happy with their purchase can leave a lasting impression.

Technology also offers multiple avenues to infuse care into various touch-points. Personalized recommendations, AI chatbots that offer instant support, and mobile apps that enhance usability – all these are examples of how technology can be leveraged to deliver care-infused experiences.

Ultimately, infusing care into every touchpoint is about moving from a transaction-centric mindset to a relationship-centric one. It's about recognizing that every interaction, no matter how small, contributes to the overall customer experience. And it's about consistently demonstrating to customers that their satisfaction, needs, and success are the driving force behind every business decision. This is the pathway to creating a customer journey based on care that extends far beyond the call centre.

In today's hyper-competitive marketplace, businesses are increasingly recognizing that transactional relationships with customers are no longer sufficient. Customers are not just seeking products or services; they are seeking experiences that make them feel valued and respected. This is where adopting a care-centric approach can truly set a business apart and create a deep-seated impact that spans over the long term. Care can be the catalyst that fosters loyalty, builds trust, and cultivates long-lasting relationships.

Loyalty cannot be bought; it has to be earned. When a business demonstrates genuine care at every touchpoint, customers start to see the business as a partner rather than just a service provider. They are more likely to stick around, even in a market where alternatives abound. In practical terms, this could mean repeat business, referrals, and a solid customer base that serves as the foundation for sustainable growth.

Trust, on the other hand, is an invaluable currency in today's world. With information readily available at their fingertips, customers are more discerning than ever. They seek transparency, authenticity, and honesty from the businesses they interact with. When a business upholds integrity as a part of its care-centric approach, it builds trust with its customers. For instance, by being transparent about pricing, admitting to mistakes and rectifying them earnestly, or openly communicating during times of crisis, a business sends a powerful message that it values honesty over short-term gains.

Moreover, trust and loyalty combined lead to the cultivation of long-lasting relationships. These relationships are not one-sided; they thrive on mutual respect and shared values. A care-centric approach means understanding and empathizing with the challenges and needs of the customer and actively involving them in shaping the products or services. This kind of collaboration enhances the customer experience and often leads to innovation and development that benefits the business.

It is also important to note that the impact of a care-centric approach is not just external; it also resonates internally within the organization. When employees see that the business is committed to care, it often instils a sense of pride and responsibility. They are more likely to align with the company's values and become ambassadors of care themselves. This internal culture of care can further amplify the positive impact on customer relationships.

In an age where stories and experiences are shared widely through social media, a care-centric approach is not just a strategy; it's a narrative that defines the brand. A single act of genuine care can resonate with a global audience and shape the perception of the brand for years to come.

A care-centric approach is not just about customer satisfaction but about building something larger than transactions. It's about creating a community of customers who feel like they are a part of the business and who trust the business with their money, time, and emotions. In the long run, this is what defines the legacy of a business – not just the revenue, but the relationships it has nurtured through genuine care.

Integrating Technology without Sacrificing Care

In a world where technology continues to advance at a breakneck pace, integrating various technological tools in the realm of customer service and experience is not just an option; it's a necessity. However, while employing technology, businesses need to tread carefully to ensure that they enhance care rather than overshadowing or replacing the human aspect, which is indispensable.

Artificial intelligence has been at the forefront of technological innovation and is widely used to optimize customer interactions. Chatbots and virtual assistants can be incredibly efficient in handling routine queries, thereby freeing up human agents to focus on more complex and sensitive issues. They can also help gather initial information, so when a customer is eventually connected to a human representative, the representative is already informed and can provide more personalized assistance. Moreover, AI-powered analytics can provide invaluable insights into customer behaviour, preferences, and needs, which can be instrumental in tailoring services and products.

Another technology that can significantly enhance care is Customer Relationship Management (CRM) systems. These systems can keep track of customer interactions over time, which enables service representatives to have a history of the customer's past experiences. This facilitates more informed and considerate interactions, as the representatives do not treat the customers as strangers but as valued individuals with a history with the company.

Extending the example of a CRM, it's crucial to understand that while the system can streamline and organize information, it doesn't possess the innate human attributes necessary for genuine care. Just as a pot doesn't make a good meal, a CRM can't transform a bad seller into a good one. This brings into focus the indispensable role of the human element.

A seller, akin to a chef, brings their unique personality, intuition, experience, and empathy to the table. With their artistry and passion, a chef can transform the simplest ingredients into a sumptuous meal. Similarly, a skilled seller, armed with sincerity and the intention to care, can build lasting relationships and create value for the customer. This is where the magic happens – in the personal touch, understanding human emotions, and genuine desire to serve.

Here, the principle of care is at the forefront. Like a CRM, technology is a powerful enabler, but it must be used to augment human skills, not replace them. It is in the combination of advanced tools and the human touch that the most potent customer experiences are crafted.

This reinforces the notion that genuine care cannot be automated or replicated by technology alone. It is born out of the depths of human empathy and commitment to serving others. As professionals and businesses, the challenge lies in harnessing the capabilities of technology while simultaneously nurturing and elevating the human qualities that form the foundation of care.

Businesses mustn't fall into the trap of letting technology take over completely. The human touch is irreplaceable and holds immense value. No matter how advanced a chatbot is, it cannot replicate the empathy, compassion, and understanding that a human being can offer. Especially in sensitive situations or when a customer is distressed, the comforting presence of another human being can be far more reassuring and effective than the most sophisticated AI.

This is why it is vital to strike a balance. Technology should be viewed as an enabler that can facilitate and support the process of care but not as a replacement for human connection. Businesses need to be mindful of the limitations of technology and must know when to escalate an interaction to a human representative.

Training and guiding human staff members in understanding when and how to intervene in technology-driven interactions is essential. For instance, if a chatbot is not able to resolve a customer's issue or if the customer is showing signs of frustration, a human representative should promptly step in.

Furthermore, businesses must ensure that they communicate openly with customers about how technology is being used to enhance their experience. This helps set the right expectations and conveys that the business is employing technology with the customer's best interest in mind.

Integrating technology without sacrificing care is a delicate balancing act. It requires a thoughtful approach that recognizes the strengths and limitations of technology while never losing sight of the central role that human connection plays in care. It is about harmoniously blending efficiency and empathy, innovation and compassion, to create customer experiences that resonate on a deeper level.

Reflecting upon Chapter 4, it's evident that leaving crucial aspects like customer care to chance can be detrimental to a business. A business that lacks clear design principles concerning the customer's experience is essentially playing a high-stakes game with its future. Thus, the creation and adherence to a growth manifesto becomes essential. This manifesto serves as a navigational tool, enabling businesses to strategically define the role of human engagement and care in their growth trajectories.

One of the cornerstones of this manifesto should be the conscious and intentional incorporation of human care in customer experiences. At the C-level, decisions need to be made about how human care is integrated into customer touchpoints. For instance, does the company's website provide avenues for real human assistance when required, or does it keep the customer trapped in an endless loop of automated responses?

It's important to note that incorporating human care does not necessarily mean deploying a battalion of human resources to address issues; it's about being decisive about the level of human care the business wants to offer and ensuring that this care is embedded into the DNA of the company's culture.

Furthermore, care should be considered more holistically, beyond just human interaction. The entire customer journey should be a testament to the company's commitment to care. This requires asking pivotal questions: Has the customer journey been tailored to the specific target market? Are all touchpoints within this journey necessary? Does it strike the right balance between simplicity and attention to the customer's needs?

A well-crafted customer journey that exhibits genuine care often results from an organization that has ingrained these values into its culture and design principles. Such a company employs technology not as a substitute for the human touch but as a facilitator that enhances and streamlines the experience. By ensuring that care remains at the core of all interactions and experiences, businesses can build lasting relationships with their customers and foster an environment in which both the company and its clientele thrive. This harmonization of technology and human care is pivotal in redefining customer experiences for the modern age.

Beyond individual interactions, cultivating relationships through networking is a powerful aspect of integrating care in customer experiences. This begins with building professional bonds which aren't merely transactional. Approaching professional relationships with an authentic intention to grow, learn, and share can cultivate bonds based on mutual respect and trust. Additionally, it's important to understand that personal connections based on shared interests and values can often evolve into meaningful professional relationships. A true culture of care emerges when personal and professional connections are nurtured through genuine interaction.

Moreover, contributing to the growth of others is a vital facet of networking. This involves sharing knowledge, providing mentorship, and extending support to peers in their professional careers. A culture of care is built on the foundations of reciprocity; it strengthens the network and creates an environment where care is valued and practised.

Maintaining the connections that have been fostered is equally essential. This involves continuous communication and genuine investment in the growth of the relationship. It requires one to be present, supportive, and, most importantly, consistent in caring.

The role of care in customer experiences should not be episodic; rather, it must be an ongoing practice. This calls for a commitment to continuously reassess how to better serve our clients, peers, and partners. It's a call for continuity in care to ensure the sustainability and adaptability of relationships through the ever-evolving landscape of business.

Care is not a superficial or temporary endeavour but a long-term commitment. This commitment is integral to building and sustaining lasting relationships, ensuring customer satisfaction, and achieving overall success. In a world where technology is omnipresent, let us not forget the unparalleled value of human touch and employ technology in ways that enhance, rather than replace, genuine care. Through the intentional integration of care in our professional lives, we serve as humans first, offering depth and richness to customer experiences that technology alone could never achieve.

Chapter 10

Reimagining Client Experiences

Embracing Client-Centric Innovation

In reimagining customer experiences, the first principle that businesses need to internalize is being energized by the customer. This may seem like an oft-repeated mantra in the business world, but its essence is profound. At the heart of innovation lies the understanding and fulfilment of customer needs.

These needs can be categorized into two main types: "gain" needs and "pain" needs. Gain needs encompass aspirations for a better future, new possibilities, and improvements. In contrast, pain needs are driven by the desire to avoid negative consequences such as financial loss, reputational damage, or operational inefficiencies.

Understanding and prioritizing these needs is paramount. Innovating for a customer motivated by a vision for a better tomorrow is different from innovating for a customer trying to solve a critical problem. The approach, communication, and solutions should align with the type and gravity of the customer's needs.

But, understanding alone is not enough; empathy plays an equally critical role. This understanding and empathy should be the energizing force behind innovation. It should be the impetus that drives businesses to think outside the box, challenge the status quo, and develop solutions that resonate deeply with customers.

What is particularly exciting about being energized by the customer is that it can lead to novel solutions even under resource constraints. When a business is

DOI: 10.4324/9781032684895-13

genuinely passionate about solving customer needs, this passion often translates into creativity and ingenuity. This is where the phrase "necessity is the mother of invention" rings true. Resource constraints can, counterintuitively, become a catalyst for innovation, forcing businesses to be more agile, efficient, and imaginative in problem-solving.

Moreover, it's crucial to realize that not all customer needs are equal, so they shouldn't be treated with a one-size-fits-all approach. Businesses must be able to rank their response following the gravity of the customer's need. By doing this, businesses can allocate their resources and efforts more effectively, ensuring that the most critical needs are addressed promptly and appropriately.

When businesses are energized by understanding and empathizing with customer needs, they set the stage for client-centric innovation. This innovation is not just about introducing new products or services; it is about reshaping the entire customer experience in a way that is deeply connected to the customer's realities and aspirations and doing so with zeal and creativity, irrespective of the resources at hand.

Resource constraints are often viewed as barriers to innovation and growth. However, when approached with a positive mindset, these constraints can actually serve as catalysts that propel businesses to think more creatively and foster innovation. This phenomenon, often referred to as "frugal innovation," is about doing more with less. It is about finding efficient solutions to problems while operating within the confines of limited resources.

A striking example of how constraints can lead to extraordinary customer experiences can be observed in India. In a country where resources are often scarce, the sheer need to cater to customer demands has led to some incredibly resourceful and innovative solutions. One example is the tailoring industry. Imagine a business traveller on a tight schedule in need of a custom-made suit. Traditional tailoring would take days if not weeks. However, in Mumbai, India, it is not uncommon for tailors to provide a service where they will take measurements, tailor the garment, and have it hand-delivered to your hotel room in hours, even if it's 2.00 a.m. This level of customer service is almost unthinkable in many parts of the world but directly results from the tailor's ability to innovate within constraints.

Another example from India is the "Dabbawalas" of Mumbai. These individuals have created a lunchbox delivery and return system that is renowned for its reliability and precision, despite operating in an environment of high population density and limited infrastructure. The Dabbawalas have leveraged their constraints to build a highly efficient and low-cost supply chain that business schools around the world now study.

These examples highlight how constraints can lead to new ways of thinking, ultimately resulting in innovative solutions that meet customer needs and often exceed their expectations. Rather than viewing constraints as insurmountable obstacles, they can be embraced as challenges that can be creatively and resourcefully overcome.

This requires a shift in mindset. Businesses need to stop seeing constraints purely as limitations and start seeing them as opportunities for innovation. It involves fostering a culture that encourages problem-solving, adaptability, and a deep understanding of customer needs.

Moreover, technology can often play a critical role in turning constraints into opportunities. Through the strategic deployment of technology, businesses can optimize operations, enhance communication, and provide services and products in ways that were previously inconceivable.

Ultimately, embracing constraints is about refusing to accept the status quo and continuously pushing the boundaries of what is possible. By adopting a mindset that views constraints as opportunities to innovate, businesses can create value for their customers and achieve sustainable growth.

The crux of client-centric innovation lies in creating more with less. In an age where resources can often be limited, especially for start-ups and small businesses, the true essence of innovation is to make minimal resources work effectively to create solutions that pack immense value for the customer. It's critical to recognize that simply creating something new does not translate into value creation for the customer.

Customer-centric innovation ensures that what is created aligns seamlessly with what the customer truly values and does not impose solutions that may not have real utility for the customer. Furthermore, the experience offered to customers should not be dictated by resource constraints, but rather by the intrinsic value delivered through innovative solutions.

An integral part of making the most of limited resources is to strategically configure technologies for maximum impact. This entails creatively combining and configuring different technologies to accomplish results that might otherwise seem out of reach. For instance, integrating a chatbot with a CRM system can enable businesses to respond to customer queries promptly and ensure that responses are personalized based on customer history and preferences.

Similarly, combining data analytics with customer feedback tools can help businesses anticipate customer needs and tailor their offerings accordingly. The key is to view various technologies not in isolation but as parts of a larger ecosystem that can be dynamically configured to create a seamless and enriched customer experience. It is also important to remain open to continuous experimentation and adaptation in technology configurations to meet customers' evolving needs.

Finally, at the intersection of care and innovation lies the heart of client-centricity. The driving force behind all technological innovations should be genuine care for the customer. This goes beyond simply utilizing technology to create efficiencies; it's about reimagining the customer experience in high-quality and resource-efficient ways. Genuine care can lead businesses to question existing norms and consider radical approaches to customer service.

It can lead to innovation that doesn't just incrementally improve the customer experience but completely redefines it. Moreover, care and innovation must go hand in hand with a feedback loop that continually evaluates customer feedback to ensure that innovation remains aligned with customer expectations and desires. Embracing client-centric innovation means always putting the customer at the heart of all decision-making processes and leveraging technology creatively and resourcefully to deliver unparalleled value.

Redefining the Buying Experience

After having emphasized the importance of innovation and understanding customer needs, it is imperative to address how products are delivered to the customers. This is where go-to-market (GTM) innovation comes into play. GTM is a crucial phase in a product's lifecycle and involves strategies employed to deliver the product to its target market. The efficiency and creativity employed in GTM can significantly impact a product's adoption and success.

Take, for instance, a simple product like sneakers. If the sneakers are readily available and delivered to the customer's doorstep, it facilitates convenience, contributing to the product's success. However, if the same sneakers are available only at a remote location with limited stock, the inconvenience can hinder adoption, even though the product remains unchanged.

Traditional GTM strategies focused on maximizing efficiency and simplicity for the customer, often employing creative methods to make the best use of resources. However, in the present era, technology has emerged as a powerful ally in GTM innovation. Digitalization allows businesses to reimagine how they connect with customers and bring products to them. It enables convenient, efficient, and highly personalized methods of delivering products.

In crafting an effective GTM digitalization strategy, businesses must be well-versed in the available technologies and how they can be leveraged. Understanding the interoperability of various layers of enterprise software, the role of data analytics in understanding customer preferences, and the potential of AI-driven personalized recommendations can be crucial. For instance, an e-commerce platform can use data analytics to suggest products based on a customer's browsing history, while chatbots can provide immediate customer support.

Earlier in the book, we reviewed the concept of empowering the customer citing Uber and Airbnb as examples. These companies haven't reinvented the wheel in terms of the services they offer; ridesharing and accommodation were not new concepts. However, what they did innovate was the way these services were delivered to the customer. They streamlined the process through technological platforms, adding convenience, efficiency, and a customer-focused approach. This dramatically increased the adoption of these services.

Notably, Uber and Airbnb focus on optimizing the GTM process without really developing the core products of ridesharing and accommodation. This underscores the transformative potential of GTM digitalization in breathing new life into even conventional, legacy products and services. Businesses must, therefore, not only focus on product innovation but also embrace the boundless possibilities that GTM digitalization offers. This involves continuous learning and adaptation as technology evolves to ensure that products are not just innovative but are delivered in a manner that aligns with the evolving expectations and preferences of the modern customer.

In organizational structures, the responsibility of GTM digitalization typically falls under product marketing. However, product marketing is a relatively nascent domain and demands extensive skills, including market research, project management, positioning, messaging, and creating marketing content. Adding digital design and enterprise architecture to this mix can often be daunting for a conventional product marketer. As a result, the critical aspect of GTM digitalization is frequently overlooked, which is unfortunate considering its vast opportunities.

Digital technology, with its innate ability to automate and replicate processes, offers scalability that can mimic the efforts of a large workforce with a relatively smaller team. It can be a game-changer for small businesses, allowing them to compete with much larger rivals by being savvy in their GTM approach. Through the intelligent use of digital platforms, even smaller companies can deliver astounding value to their markets without breaking the bank. However, it is critical to discern what value to bring to the table. Deploying advanced digital solutions to offer something that doesn't resonate with the target market is an exercise in futility.

Revisiting the sneakers example helps illustrate this point. If the target market is teenagers, the GTM strategy might focus on engaging them through social media platforms like TikTok, perhaps by creating an engaging, fun in-app ordering process. However, if the target audience is the elderly, a different approach would be required. One could think about organizing events reminiscent of "Tupperware-parties" at senior living facilities, where freelance agents equipped with digital tools for sizing and ordering engage with the residents.

For instance, during these events, an agent could use a digital tool to scan the feet of the residents, send the dimensions to the manufacturing unit, and have sneakers with the perfect fit delivered to the residents with personalized packaging. Both these GTM strategies are underpinned by digital technology, but they are tailored to what the respective target market values.

What becomes apparent is that GTM digitalization is not just about using technology, it's about outmanoeuvring the competition by developing a unique selling proposition (USP) that resonates with the target audience (more to come in Chapter 11). The ultimate goal of GTM digitalization is to augment sales conversions by creating a potent and captivating positioning statement.

A GTM strategy can be considered successful when it enables the company to unambiguously articulate how its offering is distinctively valuable to the customer. It's about blending technology with an acute understanding of the market to create tailor-made, value-driven experiences that resonate with the specific needs and preferences of the target audience.

Every business needs to critically analyse and enhance the customer's purchasing experience. Businesses can focus on streamlining each aspect by breaking down this experience into its essential components – payment, ordering, delivery, costing, access, selection, and tailoring. A simple questionnaire can prove immensely valuable for businesses in this regard: How effortless is the payment process? How convenient is it for customers to place orders? What about the delivery mechanism, pricing accessibility, product variety, and customization options? Reflecting on these queries can shed light on areas of the buying experience that necessitate improvement.

In the contemporary era, digital platforms have revolutionized the ease of conducting transactions. Customers today expect and are accustomed to a seamless buying experience, and businesses that fail to meet these expectations risk losing customers to competitors that do. While existing customer loyalty may temporarily protect a business, attracting new clientele will become increasingly challenging unless the enterprise actively seeks to reinvent its purchasing experience.

Digital technologies provide an invaluable toolset for reimagining the buying process. By employing these technologies astutely, businesses can create an incredibly efficient and enjoyable purchasing experience. In some cases, the convenience of the buying process could serve as a unique selling point, giving businesses an edge over their competitors.

The scope for innovation in the buying process is boundless. For instance, businesses can integrate alternative payment methods such as Bitcoin. Automation can be leveraged to streamline the ordering process by leveraging data on customer preferences and behaviours. Instead of restricting delivery to traditional means, businesses could consider deploying specialists to assist customers in using the product for the first time. Dynamic pricing models can be introduced based on product performance or other parameters.

It is essential to recognize that while the possibilities are endless, the key is selective and strategic implementation. The focus should be on introducing changes that resonate with the target market and align with their values and expectations. By doing so, businesses enhance the customer's purchasing experience and position themselves as customer-centric innovators, adept at leveraging digital technologies for maximal impact. This, in turn, can lead to increased customer satisfaction, loyalty, and, ultimately, business growth.

The synergy between GTM innovation, especially digitalization, and the redefinition of the buying process is a cornerstone in the quest to reimagine client experiences. The GTM approach is integral to how products or services are presented and made accessible to the consumer. When innovation is woven into this fabric, it paves the way for customer-centric strategies that align product availability with the convenience and preferences of the target market.

Digitalization, in particular, has emerged as a powerful enabler in this landscape. By incorporating digital tools and platforms into the GTM strategy, businesses can achieve a level of efficiency and customization previously unattainable. From facilitating various payment methods to automating orders based on consumer behaviour, digitalization is an expansive canvas on which businesses can paint their GTM strategies.

Redefining the buying process is a natural extension of GTM digitalization. As customers' expectations evolve, so too must the journey from their decision to make a purchase through the actual acquisition of the product or service. Digitalization helps refine this journey, allowing for flexibility, speed, and convenience tailored to individual preferences. This holistic approach goes beyond just selling a product; it entails an immersive experience that fosters connection and loyalty.

In essence, reimagining client experiences is the confluence of innovatively crafted GTM strategies and a redefined buying process, both empowered by digitalization. It is about more than just transactions; it is about creating meaningful engagements with customers. This requires a deep understanding of the customer's needs, preferences, and expectations and then leveraging technology to create a seamless and enriching experience.

Businesses need to remember that this is not a one-time effort but an ongoing process. The market and technologies are in a constant state of flux. Successful businesses will stay agile, continually evaluate the efficacy of their GTM strategies, and remain receptive to adapting their buying processes.

Ultimately, in the dynamic interplay of GTM innovation, digitalization, and the buying process, lies the opportunity for businesses to meet customer expectations and exceed them. By harnessing these elements with acuity and care, businesses can craft exceptional client experiences that differentiate them in the marketplace, drive customer satisfaction, and propel sustainable growth.

Breaking Norms and Slaying Sacred Cows

In the ever-evolving landscape of customer experiences, sometimes the key to innovation lies in questioning the very fabric of established norms. One exciting way to foster this spirit of inquisitiveness and creativity is through the "What If?" game, a playful yet potent brainstorming technique that challenges the status quo by posing rule-breaking questions. This seemingly simple game can be a catalyst for ground-breaking innovations by encouraging minds to wander into territories they might not otherwise explore.

Cultivating a culture where the "sacred cows" can be questioned is vital. Sacred cows refer to untouchable beliefs, practices, or traditions often held above questioning or criticism. However, progress demands that these cows not be so sacred, and that the norms be scrutinized for their relevance and efficiency in the present context. A culture that allows for such scrutiny becomes fertile ground for unconventional, yet possibly revolutionary ideas.

Let's delve into some examples of "What if?" questions that can prompt thinking outside the box and potentially reimagine service models:

"What if we could deliver products to consumers before they even realize they need them?"

"What if our customers could customize every aspect of the product in real-time?"

"What if no human intervention was needed at any point in the customer journey?"

"What if the customers only paid for the exact amount of service or product they used, down to the smallest unit?"

These questions, among countless others, serve as igniters to brainstorming sessions. They encourage lateral thinking and open up avenues for discussions that may not arise within the confines of traditional thinking. It's important to note that not all ideas generated through the "What If?" game will be feasible or even practical. However, even the wildest ideas can sometimes lead to insights that can be shaped into innovative solutions. Breaking norms and slaying sacred cows is not about recklessness; it's about giving yourself the freedom to explore, innovate, and potentially, redefine the paradigms of customer experience.

Once the spark of a compelling idea is ignited through the "What If?" game, the next challenge lies in fanning that spark into a roaring flame of reality. This is where technology can be a significant ally. Despite the seemingly outrageous or ambitious nature of some ideas, technology's rapid evolution and democratization often provide the means to turn the impossible into the feasible.

One key element in this transformation journey is to avoid dismissing ideas prematurely due to perceived impossibilities or constraints. The history of innovation is replete with examples of ideas that initially seemed implausible, if not downright impossible, yet eventually revolutionized industries and customer experiences. Therefore, every idea deserves to be explored for its potential, no matter how outlandish it may initially appear.

In this process of exploration, reverse engineering can be an invaluable tool. It involves starting with the innovative idea and working backwards to identify the necessary technological and resourceful means required to execute it. In other words, instead of thinking, "We have these resources. What can we do with them?" the question becomes, "We have this idea. What resources or technologies do we need to realize it?" This approach fosters a problem-solving mindset that seeks to find ways to make things work rather than reasons they won't.

Imagine, for example, an idea generated from the "What If?" game: "What if customers could interact with our product in a virtual environment before purchasing?" Instead of dismissing this as a futuristic fantasy, a company could leverage emerging technologies like augmented or virtual reality to make this experience a reality. Or consider a more complex question, like "What if our products could evolve based on the user's changing needs?" This could lead to exploring artificial intelligence, machine learning, or Internet of Things technologies that allow products to learn from usage patterns and adapt accordingly.

The trick, however, is in the balance between imagination and execution. Ideas are only as good as their implementation, no matter how ground-breaking. Therefore, while the "What If?" game allows us to dream big and question norms, the real magic lies in turning those dreams into tangible experiences that add value to the customer and redefine how businesses operate.

As exhilarating as it is to bring forth a breakthrough innovation, it's crucial to recognize that innovation is not a one-time event but a continuous journey. The landscape of customer needs, preferences, and market conditions is in perpetual flux. What might be a ground-breaking innovation today could become the norm, or even obsolete, tomorrow. This dynamic nature of markets and customer expectations necessitates a commitment to continuous evolution and adaptation.

Cultivating a culture of continuous learning is paramount. Companies should foster environments where curiosity is encouraged and learning is viewed as an ongoing process. This culture should permeate all levels of the organization. Just as products and services need to evolve, so do the skills and knowledge of the people creating and delivering them. Regular training, workshops, and a focus on skill development are critical components of this learning culture.

Furthermore, customer feedback should be the lifeblood of adaptation efforts. Listening to customers and incorporating their feedback into the innovation process ensures that the company remains aligned with their evolving needs and expectations. Active engagement with customers through surveys, user testing, and direct communications offers invaluable insights that can drive the next wave of innovation.

In addition to being in tune with customers, companies must remain vigilant and adaptable to broader market trends and shifts. This means monitoring competitors, technological advancements, regulatory changes, and other external factors that could impact the business. Staying agile, with the ability to pivot quickly in response to these changes, is a critical asset in maintaining a position of leadership and innovation.

A culture that embraces change rather than fearing it is better positioned to capitalize on new opportunities as they arise. This receptivity to change should be ingrained in the organization's DNA. It requires leadership open to questioning the status quo and teams empowered to explore new approaches.

Ultimately, reimagining customer experiences through innovation is a never-ending cycle of evolution. Companies can achieve new heights of customer satisfaction, efficiency, and market leadership with each iteration. By staying agile, continuously learning, and keeping the lines of communication open with customers, companies can ensure that their innovation efforts remain relevant and impactful in a world that never stands still.

UNDERSTAND HUMANITY

4

As we find ourselves more enmeshed in the virtual world, Part 4 brings the indispensability of the physical, "real" world to the forefront. This part explores the essence of humanity, the motives that drive decision-makers, and the significance of effective positioning in the tangible realm. It's a wake-up call, urging readers not to lose grip on the actual world where life truly unfolds. Within this part, strategies are provided for businesses and individuals to harness their understanding of human nature for positioning products, services, and themselves in a manner that resonates deeply. This section is a compass to navigate the delicate balance between the virtual and the real. In an age that is easy to get swept away by the digital current, reclaiming reality is the anchor that ensures sustained relevance and fulfilment.

DOI: 10.4324/9781032684895-14

Chapter 11

A Theoretical Grounding

The Need for a Theoretical Framework

In the fervour of innovation and the haste to bring products and services to an ever-evolving market, there's a critical component that often gets neglected: positioning. In this chapter, we reconnect with our north star set out in Chapter 1. The foundation for this chapter rests on the understanding that the human touch is still king, despite the inroads made by AI-driven interfaces.

One must recognize that the market is not a static entity. It's alive, constantly changing, with tastes, preferences, and needs that evolve at breakneck speed. Today's market is no longer just about fulfilling a need; it is about resonance. Your product or service must strike a chord, evoke emotions, and create bonds beyond the transactional. People look for what reflects their values, aspirations, and identities. Your positioning should, therefore, be a reflection of not just what your product does but what it stands for in the hearts and minds of the consumers.

Let's underline the term "growth." In the context of this book, growth encompasses a wide spectrum – it's personal, professional, and societal. How does positioning play into this?

Positioning is, at its core, an understanding and an articulation of where you stand in the marketplace relative to others. It's about carving a niche, a space you can call your own. It's about ensuring that this space is where your audience wants to be. That's where the resonance comes in. Positioning is a bridge between what you have to offer and what the market seeks. When done right, positioning leads to growth – a growth that's sustainable, meaningful, and enriching.

DOI: 10.4324/9781032684895-15

In the Age of AI, inundated with data and automated analytics, there's a common misconception that numbers can tell the whole story. While quantitative data is incredibly valuable, it doesn't replace the qualitative human insight. Delving into the human psyche, understanding motives and values, and empathetically connecting to the emotional aspects of consumption are irreplaceable facets of positioning.

This requires a focus on human observation and interaction. It involves understanding stories, histories, and cultures. It's about knowing that behind every data point, there's a human face with a narrative. It's these narratives that often hold the keys to successful positioning.

The marketplace today is more fluid than ever. Technological advancements, cultural shifts, and global events can rapidly change the landscape. In such an environment, rigidity can be fatal. Your positioning must be flexible and adaptive. It should evolve as the market evolves. This requires an ongoing dialogue with the market, and a continuous effort to listen, understand, and adapt.

With the proliferation of digital platforms, the line between the virtual and the real often gets blurred. However, even in the virtual space, human connection remains vital. It's crucial to recognize that whether you are engaging with your audience online or offline, the principles of human connection remain the same.

Virtual platforms offer new ways and means to engage, but the fundamental need for meaningful, value-based connection persists. Your positioning must navigate this duality, anchoring in the real while leveraging the virtual.

The theoretical framework for positioning in the AI age is thus multidimensional. It combines an understanding of your offerings, an empathetic insight into the human aspects of the market, an adaptable approach that evolves with changing dynamics, and a duality that navigates the virtual and the real.

Positioning is not a one-time effort. It's an ongoing process of alignment and realignment, ensuring that you stay relevant and connected. It's about realizing that in the buzzing marketplace, the human touch, the genuine care, and the value-driven approach will set you apart.

As you move forward, wield this understanding as a compass. Let it guide your journey through the intricacies of the marketplace in the AI age. Position your endeavours not just for financial success but also for creating lasting value that resonates through lives, relationships, and communities. This is the path to holistic growth. This is the essence of mastering the art of positioning in the Age of Agency.

In the modern market, there's a certain allure to agility and quick decisions. The fast-paced nature of the marketplace might give the impression that speed is of the essence. This can lead to a temptation to rely on gut feelings or make ad-hoc positioning decisions without any structural backbone. However, this approach is akin to building a house on shifting sands. Without a solid foundation, even the most well-intentioned efforts can crumble. Here, we will discuss the importance of employing a tried-and-tested theoretical framework for positioning and why due diligence is more critical than ever.

Guesswork or instinctual decision-making can sometimes yield results, but it's essentially a gamble. When you rely on guesswork, you put yourself at the mercy of external factors. You might be right today and wrong tomorrow. Moreover, this approach lacks scalability and repeatability. You cannot consistently replicate success without a framework to understand what worked and why.

Guesswork is transient and volatile; it doesn't lend itself to enduring solutions. This lack of stability can be disastrous in a world that is already in constant flux. The absence of a theoretical framework means that your positioning lacks anchoring in principles and data, making it susceptible to being swayed by every wind of change.

A theoretical framework brings stability and structure to your positioning. It acts as the bedrock upon which your strategies are built. Employing a framework ensures that your positioning is not just a spur-of-the-moment decision but is based on solid research, analysis, and tested principles.

The theoretical framework acts as a filter, helping you sift through the noise of the market. It ensures that your positioning aligns with both the internal goals of your endeavour and the external realities of the market.

This is not to say that a theoretical framework makes your positioning rigid. On the contrary, a good framework allows for adaptation but ensures that this adaptation is systematic and not haphazard.

In a world that values sustainability and longevity, robust solutions are paramount. A robust solution is one that not only addresses the immediate concerns but is also resilient to future challenges.

Let's revisit the Washington Monument exercise from Chapter 3. The exercise illustrated the importance of addressing the root cause of a problem instead of just dealing with the symptoms. This principle is highly applicable in positioning. A theoretical framework assists you in digging deeper, understanding the underlying currents of the market, and positioning yourself in a way that addresses these foundational aspects.

Focusing on the root causes and fundamental factors makes your positioning enduring. It's not swayed by temporary trends but is aligned with the deeper movements of the market. Due diligence is often seen as a time-consuming effort. However, its value cannot be overstated. When you invest time and resources in properly researching and understanding the market, this investment compounds over time.

With due diligence, you gain insights that can shape your current positioning and give you the tools to navigate future challenges. You become adept at reading the market, understanding its nuances, and making informed decisions.

Moreover, due diligence enhances credibility and trustworthiness. When your audience realizes that your positioning is based on a deep understanding and a genuine effort to align with their values and needs, they are more likely to trust and engage with you.

Employing a tried-and-tested theoretical framework for positioning is an investment in stability, robustness, and enduring value. In a world of constant changes and uncertainties, this framework acts as your compass, keeping you oriented and grounded.

It's about marrying agility with solidity. Being able to move swiftly but not recklessly. Being adaptive but not fickle. It is this balance that a theoretical framework offers. As you chart your path in the Age of Agency, let this framework be your guiding star and the mast that holds your sails as you navigate the ever-changing seas of the marketplace.

In a world constantly inundated with new ideas, technologies, and methodologies, it's tempting to be enamoured by the shiny new objects that beckon from every corner. Especially when it comes to marketing and positioning in the Age of AI, there is no shortage of modern techniques and technologies vying for attention. However, it is crucial to recognize that the fundamental essence of human interaction, value creation, and positioning does not change with the advent of new technologies. AI can enhance our capabilities but doesn't replace the foundations upon which effective positioning is built.

In light of this understanding, I have chosen to illuminate our path with the wisdom emanating from two enduring classics that have withstood the test of time. These admired texts are steeped in insights and remind us of the enduring nature of certain principles that remain relevant across ages.

The first text is E. Jerome McCarthy's seminal work, *Basic Marketing*. This is not just any marketing book; it's a watershed moment in the history of marketing thought. In this extraordinary text, McCarthy introduced the world to the concept of the marketing mix, which came to be famously known as the Four Ps of Marketing: Product, Price, Place, and Promotion.

Why is this so foundational? Because it encapsulates the essence of what it means to position a product or service in the market. It compels us to think not only about the product itself but also about how it's priced, distributed, and communicated to the target audience. This holistic view ensures that all facets of marketing are aligned and working in concert.

In an era of AI, where data analytics and ML can sometimes bewilder us into a state of myopia, focusing on one aspect and neglecting others, McCarthy's marketing mix serves as a timeless reminder to see the bigger picture. It helps us remember that successful positioning results from a harmonious integration of multiple elements. AI can enhance each of these elements, but the fundamental structure provided by the Four Ps remains invaluable.

The second treasure I have chosen to delve into is *Reality in Advertising* by Rosser Reeves. In this ground-breaking book, Reeves introduced the world to the concept of the unique selling proposition or USP.

The USP is a critical element of positioning. It involves identifying and communicating a unique benefit or feature that distinguishes a product or service from its competitors. In a world that's increasingly crowded and competitive, the ability to identify and articulate a USP is more critical than ever.

AI technologies have provided new avenues for product customization and personalization, which may give the impression that the concept of USP is becoming diluted. However, this is not the case. While AI enables us to create more tailored offerings, the need to communicate a distinct value proposition remains as vital as ever. Rosser Reeves's concept of the USP helps us cut through the clutter and focus on what truly differentiates us in the market.

These classic texts were chosen for their timeless wisdom and to emphasize an important point – that the new does not invalidate the old. In fact, they can be symbiotic. AI and modern technology should be seen as tools that amplify our ability to execute the timeless principles outlined in these texts.

By anchoring ourselves in the tried-and-tested methodologies of *Basic Marketing* and *Reality in Advertising*, we ensure that our positioning is built on a solid foundation. The advent of AI and other technologies can accelerate and enhance our capabilities, but they do so most effectively when employed within the framework of enduring principles.

As we forge ahead, let's carry the wisdom of the ages in one hand and the tools of modernity in the other. Together, they provide us with a potent combination that is well equipped to navigate the complexities and challenges of positioning in the ever-evolving marketplace.

Unpacking the Frameworks

As we venture into applying the timeless frameworks elucidated by E. Jerome McCarthy and Rosser Reeves, it is imperative to underscore an elemental truth – positioning does not exist in isolation. It is the consequence of a well-thought-out growth strategy. Before we delve into the intricacies of applying the marketing mix and the unique selling proposition, let us pause and consider the foundational bedrock upon which these frameworks must be built: the growth strategy.

In a tumultuous and highly competitive marketplace, often characterized as hostile and brimming with challenges and adversaries, the beacon that guides our positioning efforts is our growth strategy. There is a prevailing discourse on the close-knit relationship between growth and positioning, and rightly so, but the depth of this relationship is crucial to understand. Positioning is not an end in itself; it is a vehicle through which growth strategies are realized.

A growth strategy encompasses an organisation's overarching objectives, tactics, and methods to expand its market share, customer base, or revenue. It is the roadmap that outlines how a product, service, or organization will evolve over time, ensuring sustainability amidst shifting market dynamics.

Positioning, in this context, is about crafting a unique space in the minds of the consumers and the market at large, which resonates with the value proposition of your product or service. It's about aligning perception with the innate strengths and value that your offering embodies. This alignment is what paves the way for the realization of the growth strategy.

It's important to understand that without a clear growth strategy, positioning efforts might be scattered, inconsistent, or misaligned with the true value that an offering holds. Conversely, a growth strategy without effective positioning is like a ship without a rudder, directionless amidst the tempestuous waters of the market.

As we unpack the frameworks, it is essential to heed E. Jerome McCarthy's astute observation from the third edition of *Basic Marketing* that "The Marketing Manager does not work in a vacuum. He must consider much more than just the four Ps and choosing target markets." This statement accentuates the necessity of understanding the context in which one operates, both in business and career. Developing a sound understanding of the environment is crucial to craft strategies and position oneself effectively.

Let us dissect the significance of a few of the environmental variables mentioned by McCarthy and construe a robust argument for why this understanding is indispensable.

Understanding the cultural and social environment is pivotal as it forms the undercurrents that shape consumer behaviour, preferences, and decision-making. Culture imbibes values, beliefs, customs, and norms, which heavily influence what products or services are valued within a community. Moreover, social dynamics such as family, friends, and social media can significantly impact consumer choices. By understanding cultural and social nuances, a business or individual can tailor offerings to resonate with the target audience, ensuring they are both relevant and valued.

The political and legal environment is multifaceted, encompassing government policies, regulations, political stability, and legal requirements. Navigating this landscape is crucial because it establishes the parameters within which a business or career can operate. A change in government policy or the introduction of new legislation can have far-reaching consequences. For instance, stringent data protection laws can impact how companies handle consumer data. Being proactive and being aware of political and legal environments allow for better risk management and compliance, safeguarding against potential legal disputes or unfavourable governmental interventions.

The economic environment is an amalgamation of inflation rates, unemployment levels, economic growth, and consumer spending habits. These elements have a direct bearing on both business performance and career prospects. For example, during an economic downturn, consumers might cut back on spending, necessitating businesses to adapt their offerings or marketing strategies. Likewise, a booming economy might offer lucrative career opportunities. Therefore, understanding the economic environment is cardinal for making informed decisions that capitalize on opportunities and mitigate risks.

These variables are interwoven and collectively shape the context in which businesses and careers operate. Ignoring any of these environmental aspects can result in misaligned strategies and missed opportunities.

For example, a business venturing into a new market must understand the economic feasibility and the cultural relevance of its products, the social channels through which to engage customers, and the regulatory compliance required.

For individuals, understanding the environment can be pivotal for career development. Grasping the cultural and social dynamics can enhance networking, comprehending economic trends can inform career choices, and being cognizant of the political landscape can facilitate advocacy and influence.

Understanding the environment is not just a supplementary skill but a fundamental keystone for effective positioning and realizing growth strategies. By blending environmental insight with the application of frameworks like the marketing mix and unique selling proposition, one can craft strategies that are not only robust but are also harmoniously attuned to the beat of the ever-evolving market dynamics.

In the current landscape, generative technologies, businesses, and individuals are churning out a formidable sea of content. The marketing realm has never before experienced such a deluge of information. It's as if we are collectively trying to satiate an unquenchable thirst for more options, information, and choices. Amidst this barrage, selecting a target market becomes a strategic move and a sanctuary for both the marketer and the consumer. It is a lighthouse in the storm, guiding the way for those seeking something tailored that speaks to them.

When E. Jerome McCarthy stressed on the importance of marketing managers selecting target customers, he highlighted the quintessence of creating meaning in a marketplace. To select a target audience is to choose to whom one's efforts will bring value. It is a commitment to understanding, serving, and elevating a specific group.

But why stop at merely selecting a target market? Why not go further? There is an art, almost a kind of magic, in embracing niche marketing. Niche marketing is the alchemy of taking specificity to its peak. It is the daring act of saying,

"This is precisely for you." In the niche, products and services can become like well-crafted letters, written with love and sent to someone yearning to read them. The essence of niche marketing lies in its ability to foster a deep bond between the product and the consumer, a bond that feels almost personal.

Imagine being a traveller lost in an unknown city, with billboards in languages you don't understand and streets filled with unfamiliar sights. Then, suddenly, you find a small cafe, and inside, your mother tongue is spoken, your traditional dishes are served, and the fragrance of your homeland fills the air. How invaluable would that place be to you? This is the power of niche marketing. It can take a piece of the chaos and make it home for someone. It builds connections that are intimate and real. It speaks to the soul.

In the Age of Agency, when generative content is at an all-time high, spray-and-pray strategies are not just ineffective, they're almost like white noise. They're the background hum that no one pays attention to. The world doesn't need more noise; it needs more music. And music happens when there's a harmony, a match between the note and the ear that's meant to hear it.

One could argue that technology has made executing spray-and-pray strategies easier. However, this ease doesn't translate to effectiveness. In a world that's becoming increasingly automated, human connection is and will remain irreplaceable. People don't just want products or services; they want echoes of their own heartbeat. They want to be seen, understood, and valued.

Niche marketing, by its very nature, requires an understanding of the complexity that makes up human desire and need. It is a reminder that behind the demographics and data are human stories. As McCarthy would argue, marketing managers must ensure their strategies are effective and ready to adapt. This adaptability is not just in response to data but also to the human experience. When strategies are adaptable, they can morph and grow just as people do.

In an era where content is abundant but connection is scarce, the audacity to be specific is revolutionary. It's not just a business strategy; it's an act of human understanding. It's the creation of spaces where values, stories, and lives can intersect in the most meaningful ways. It's about making not just a sale but a difference.

In the ever-evolving marketing landscape, the words of Rosser Reeves from his seminal work, *Reality in Advertising*, resonate with relevance, especially in the contemporary ecosystem fuelled by artificial intelligence. Reeves posited that each advertisement must make a proposition to the consumer, saying, "Buy the product, and you will get this specific benefit." The essence of this rule lies in the clarity and directness of the message. In today's digital age, consumers are bombarded with overwhelming information. AI algorithms personalize and serve advertisements at an unprecedented scale. Amidst this deluge, the importance of a clear and specific benefit cannot be overstated. Consumers, though swamped, are ever more discerning. They seek value and are likely attracted to products or services that cut through the noise with a distinct promise.

Moreover, AI's role in gathering insights means that companies now have data about consumer preferences, pain points, and aspirations. With such insights, it is even more crucial for businesses to align their offerings with what genuinely matters to their audience and to communicate it unequivocally. A company that uses data to discern a pressing need and then tailors its product to meet this need, ensuring that its advertisements highlight this benefit, essentially embraces the essence of Reeves' first rule.

Reeves' second rule states, "The proposition must be one that the competition either cannot, or does not, offer. It must be unique – either a uniqueness of the brand or a claim not otherwise made in that particular field of advertising." The mandate for uniqueness in the proposition has gained even more significance in the Age of AI. With AI-driven market research, competitors are often equally aware of the gaps in the market. However, AI can also foster a false sense of homogenization where companies might gravitate towards similar solutions based on data. Herein lies the golden opportunity for the discerning marketer. A brand that leverages its inherent strengths, values, and innovation to craft a markedly unique proposition is likely to stand out. This uniqueness could be in the form of an unprecedented feature, an exceptional experience, or an unmatched level of service. It is something that others cannot replicate easily.

In the Age of AI, brands must go the extra mile to ensure that their unique proposition is not just distinct but deeply aligned with the values and aspirations of their audience. AI algorithms may reveal trends, but human ingenuity and empathy are essential in translating these trends into meaningful offerings. Additionally, this uniqueness must be defended and nurtured. In an era where AI can speed up the development of competing products, companies must invest in continual innovation, brand-building, and community engagement to sustain their unique positioning.

Now consider the role of social media and online communities, which have become a mainstay in modern life. A strong, unique proposition reverberates through these platforms. Consumers who find an offering that resonates with their needs and values are likely to share and advocate for the product. In an age where consumer voices can be amplified, a well-crafted, unique selling proposition can gain momentum rapidly.

As we navigate through the crowded and tumultuous waters of the AI-driven market, the compass that guides a brand to its coveted treasure is the crafting of a cogent proposition that not only offers a specific benefit but does so in a way that is unparalleled and deeply resonant with the audience. Rosser Reeves' principles of a specific benefit and uniqueness are not just marketing strategies; they guide a brand towards establishing an authentic connection with its consumers and in doing so, carve out its legend in the market.

A Bridge to the Practical

In the pages that have led us to this point, we've immersed ourselves in the wisdom of two towering figures in the world of marketing: E. Jerome McCarthy, who taught us about the importance of a marketing mix through *Basic Marketing*, and Rosser Reeves, who introduced us to the concept of unique selling proposition in *Reality in Advertising*. While their words have provided us with frameworks, it's time to apply these teachings to the real world.

Let's start by revisiting McCarthy. His work insists on comprehending the cultural, social, economic, and political environments. This essentially means that to build a successful marketing strategy, we must listen. The market is akin to a living, breathing organism. It has a heartbeat, a rhythm of its own, and if we are to create value, we must first understand what the market values are. This knowledge is not merely for academic satisfaction.

It's the very soil in which our strategies must take root. Ignoring this environment is like trying to grow a tropical plant in a desert; it simply won't thrive. It's imperative to understand that markets are made up of people, and people are influenced by their surroundings. By listening to the pulse of the market, we're more informed and better equipped to make decisions that resonate with those we serve.

As for Reeves and his unique selling proposition, consider it a beacon. It's not enough to merely have a product; one must communicate its value in a compelling and distinct manner. What is it that makes your offering stand out in a crowded market? With the advent of AI, consumers today are bombarded with information. How does one break through this clutter? The USP helps create this differentiation. But, as Reeves suggests, it's not just about being different; it's about offering something that the competition either cannot or does not offer. It's this relevance and uniqueness that make a proposition magnetic.

Combining these two perspectives, it becomes evident that McCarthy and Reeves are not disparate in their outlook. They are two sides of the same coin. While McCarthy teaches us the significance of understanding the environment, which is essentially looking outward, Reeves emphasizes the importance of looking inward, honing in on what is uniquely ours to offer.

As we enter the real world, these theories must become our tools. Understanding our environment helps us identify gaps, needs, and opportunities. Crafting a unique selling proposition helps us position ourselves in a genuine and appealing way.

Imagine yourself as a craftsman. Your craft is the product or service you offer. The tools handed down to you by McCarthy and Reeves are there to ensure that your craft not only sees the light of day but shines brightly enough to be seen.

As the pages of this chapter come to a close and the anticipation for what lies ahead grows, it is crucial that you, the reader, take a moment to embrace the significance of the theoretical groundwork we've laid. The stage is set for your imminent venture into the realm of practice, but before you take that leap, allow yourself the space to reflect on the gravity of the methods discussed.

Consider it an invitation to view *Basic Marketing* and *Reality in Advertising* not as mere compendiums of marketing knowledge but as living tools for crafting meaningful strategies. These techniques demand a mindful connection to the world around you; they implore you to see beyond the walls of your office or the confines of your workspace. Ask yourself: Why does my growth strategy require me to understand my environment? What would be the consequences if I ignored the world outside?

Understanding the threads of culture, economy, and social dynamics is paramount to identifying where your contributions fit. Moreover, through this understanding, the essence of a unique selling proposition reveals itself. Without a pulse on the market's heartbeat, how can one hope to identify what is truly unique? What would make a customer turn their head?

The bridge to the practical is built on the pillars of contextual awareness and an unyielding commitment to serving the needs and desires of your audience. This holistic understanding serves as a torch, guiding you through the real world that awaits in the next chapter.

Chapter 12

The Real World

Reconnecting and Sensing

As we step into this chapter, it is essential to ground ourselves in the reality we inhabit, and what better way to do this than through a tangible, introspective exercise? This exercise, titled "Reconnecting with the Real World," aims to deepen your appreciation for the human experience and to help alleviate fears of obsolescence in the face of AI advancements. The goal is to awaken a sense of connection and observation, allowing you to perceive the everyday world with fresh eyes.

To start, grab a notebook or open a notepad on your phone. Divide a page into four sections and label them as follows: (a) what you need from the real world; (b) what others need from the real world; (c) what you can do easily that AI cannot; (d) what others can do easily, that AI cannot.

With your notepad ready, embark on your day. Here's where the exploration begins. Focus on one category at a time. Starting with category (a), engage your senses and observe your own needs. Maybe you notice the thirst that prompts you to reach for a glass of water, the comfort your slippers offer as you walk across the floor, or the space and amenities your kitchen provides. Keep it simple and stick to what you personally experience; this is about genuine observation, not overthinking.

Next, shift your focus to category (b). Watch the world around you and take note of what others need. Your eyes may be drawn to the father buying medicine at the pharmacy, a child reaching for her mother's hand across the street, or a colleague seeking a listening ear. These observations remind you that we all live interconnected lives filled with needs and desires.

 DOI: 10.4324/9781032684895-16

When you move on to category (c), you'll start to rediscover the beauty of human capabilities – ones that AI hasn't mastered. Maybe it's how you skilfully flip an omelette, the gentle touch you provide when consoling a friend, or how you negotiate a resolution in a tense meeting. These moments are testaments to the depth and adaptability of human skills.

Lastly, category (d) will allow you to observe these same qualities in the people around you. You might see a barista craft the perfect cappuccino with flair or watch a busker play an instrument with soul and passion. These observations culminate in awe and appreciation for the mesh of skills and talents that make up our collective humanity.

Engage in this exercise wholeheartedly and without judgement. It's meant to be an enriching and eye-opening experience that reaffirms the value and uniqueness of human life in a world where AI continues to make strides. Through this practice, you'll give yourself insights and a fresh perspective the next time a conversation about AI and its role in our world arises. Dive in, explore, and allow yourself to reconnect with the real world.

As individuals from various walks of life engage in this exercise, a mixture of human experience and needs unfolds. Mothers, for instance, might jot down in their notebooks the need for baby formula, diapers, a few moments of quiet, or a reassuring conversation with another parent. They may observe other mothers in the park seeking shade and benches or notice how adept they themselves are at soothing a crying child – a task no AI can replicate with the same warmth and genuine care.

Factory workers might take note of their need for reliable transportation to work, protective gear, and coffee breaks to refuel. They could witness their colleagues requiring specialized tools or sharing a laugh during lunch, a subtle reminder of the camaraderie that AI cannot participate in. They might feel a sense of pride in the deftness and precision with which they operate machinery, adapting instantly to minor hiccups.

Driving through bustling streets, taxi drivers would notice the indispensable role GPS plays in their lives and their reliance on well-maintained roads. They might observe passengers' need for quick, safe rides and observe how they offer an ear to passengers' stories or help with heavy luggage – a humane touch that an autonomous vehicle cannot offer.

In the world of accountants, the picture looks different but equally rich. An accountant might note the essential nature of their computer systems, client data, and office supplies. Observing fellow accountants grappling with complex financial problems, they realize the creative and analytical thinking that goes into resolving these issues – a blend of logic and intuition that AI has yet to fully emulate.

Similarly, engineers might need advanced software, quiet spaces for focus, and collaborative platforms. They could witness colleagues brainstorm and build upon each other's ideas, combining knowledge and creativity in ways that algorithms cannot reproduce.

The observations pour in across the globe, from the streets of New York to rural villages in Africa. The need for clean water, the comfort of a family meal, the dexterity involved in crafting artisan bread, or the skill a teacher employs to engage a room full of restless children. The list is endless and varies widely, yet there is a common thread – the irreplaceable and diverse nature of human needs and capabilities.

As the pages of notebooks and screens of notepads fill with the vibrant, varied, and heartfelt observations gathered from this exercise, there is a blossoming within the heart. A tender bud of love and admiration that grows into full bloom for oneself and for the motley crew that is humanity.

From the young mother who can calm her baby with a gentle lullaby to the aged street musician whose soulful tunes defy the passage of time, there is a realization that the human spirit is boundless. Each soul carries a universe of stories, talents, dreams, and triumphs within it. Even the individual who might seem down and out, sitting on a street corner, has a heart capable of love, hands that once held another, and a mind that has pondered the mysteries of life.

With this unfolding admiration comes a rekindling, a reconnection to the world that cradles us all. We begin to fathom the depths of our bond to the earth beneath our feet, the air that fills our lungs, and the simple miracles of everyday life. A revelation dawns that our existence is not an isolated chapter but an interlinked mix of relationships and dependencies with the world and with each other. The seeds we plant in the soil, the conversations we share over a cup of tea, and the products we exchange in marketplaces are all part of this complex mixture.

There is no denying that the rapid advancements in AI have shaken the ground beneath our feet. The uncertainty of what these synthetic intellects might mean for our place in the world is disconcerting. However, as we immerse ourselves in the richness of the real world, perspective begins to take root. Our lives are ensconced in a symphony of sensory experiences and meaningful connections, something that AI cannot replicate or replace.

We realize that AI, powerful though it may be, is still just a tool created by human hands and minds. It can help us build bridges, analyse data, and perhaps make our lives more convenient in many ways. However, it cannot feel the warmth of sunlight on a spring day nor comprehend the unspoken bond between lifelong friends. It doesn't know the thrill of an unexpected discovery or the healing power of a kind word. It's in these profoundly human experiences that our true strength lies.

As we stand at this intersection of humanity and technology, let's choose to embrace the boundless potential within ourselves and our fellow travellers in this journey of life. Much work must be done to mend, build, nurture, and create a world that fulfils the myriad needs of our kind. Let's wield AI as the tool it is, but never forget that the heart of our world is, and always will be, undeniably human. The world is real, and it's time to roll up our sleeves, with love in our hearts and dreams in our eyes, and get real.

Zooming Out to the Stark Plight of Humanity

As the gentle hum of progress continues to vibrate through the air, with the tantalizing allure of artificial intelligence reshaping countless facets of modern life, it is crucial to take a moment and zoom out. Zoom out to a broader, more encompassing panorama of the human experience, which stretches far beyond the glittering skyscrapers and digital screens. One must come to terms with a stark yet oft-overlooked reality – a large portion of humanity still grapples with the most basic of needs.

Artificial intelligence, for all its prominence in discourse and media, is still a player on a rather limited stage. It is supposed that AI technologies have permeated and influenced only a small percentage of the global population. It makes ripples in industries and communities already situated within the folds of modernization. Meanwhile, an astonishing number of souls still wander a landscape parched of basic amenities. In regions across Africa, Asia, and beyond, countless individuals wake up to a day of scouring for food, water, and shelter. The parched throats and the fragile roofs over heads speak of a primal and fundamental longing.

In places where access to clean water is a luxury and where meals are not assured, the talk of AI-driven automation and data analytics is akin to speaking an alien tongue. And yet, the heart doesn't falter in its beat, and dreams don't cease to take wing. The human spirit persists, sometimes flickering, sometimes ablaze, but ever present.

This invites a soul-searching question: In a world where our technologies promise the moon and the stars, shouldn't our creative impulses and resources be channelled towards illuminating the dark corners of human suffering? Instead of harbouring fear about AI stealing jobs of a few, shouldn't we embrace this as an opportunity to direct collective efforts towards places and people who, numbering in the millions, wait, underutilized and excluded?

Recalling the insights from Chapter 4, the boundless capability inherent in every human being, regardless of their background, surpasses that of the most advanced AI. This is a wellspring of potential that awaits nurturing and an opportunity. Combining the potential of AI with the indomitable human spirit can be the alchemy that transmutes despair into hope.

There is an imperative to reorient, to recalibrate our compasses so that the needles point towards compassion, and our maps are charted to destinations where kindling the light in a child's eye or ensuring a meal for a hungry family is the treasure sought. It's not just about AI augmenting businesses or enhancing convenience; it's about AI, hand in hand with the resilience and diversity of humanity, augmenting hope and breathing life into the very essence of our shared existence.

This is not a journey to be taken lightly, nor is it a path devoid of obstacles. But as we stand at the cusp of possibilities, the impetus for harnessing AI and human ingenuity to alleviate the plight of those less fortunate reverberates. It's time to respond. It's time to weave tales of innovation and progress, of hearts emboldened and lives transformed.

A most strange and beguiling paradox has emerged in our collective fascination and ceaseless pursuit of artificial intelligence. We stand on the cusp of a world imbued with an intelligence of our own making, an intelligence that learns, adapts, and interacts with us in ways we could scarcely have imagined a few short decades ago. Yet, as we strain our eyes towards the horizon of AI, we often overlook the vast reservoir of authentic human intelligence that surrounds us.

Our world teems with minds bursting with potential, creativity, questions, solutions, and musings that could fill a thousand libraries. Every child who looks up at the stars in wonder, every farmer who knows the language of the soil and weather, every artist who paints with a palette of human emotion carries within them an intelligence that is real, tangible, and profoundly influential.

However, this vast panorama of human intelligence is often left unattended, unnoticed, and un-nurtured. While AI algorithms are carefully trained and fine-tuned, there are minds and hearts in the corners of our world that remain shrouded in the darkness of neglect. They yearn for the light of knowledge, the warmth of understanding, and the opportunities these can bring.

This is not to suggest that the advancements in AI are in any way trivial or unnecessary. On the contrary, these innovations represent a massive advance of human ingenuity and ambition. However, they are only as valuable as the human potential they unlock, the lives they enrich, and the societal challenges they help us overcome. If AI can uplift and empower human intelligence, it becomes a tool of unimaginable power and worth.

This isn't a call for ending world hunger, although that would be a noble and worthy endeavour. Rather, this is a call to recognize and honour the fundamental needs of humans across our planet. These needs, many basic yet essential, remain unmet for an alarming number of individuals.

If our investment in AI doesn't contribute to the alleviation of these human conditions, then we must ask ourselves, why do we even bother? If the pursuit of intelligence for intelligence's sake is our goal, then we must remember that we already possess such intelligence in vast abundance. Our world is teeming with it. So, why the compulsive need to create more? Is it merely a fascination with our ability to play creator? A modern-day Frankenstein syndrome, perhaps?

The application of AI cannot and should not stop at more efficient email drafting or quicker web searches. Its potential extends far beyond these relatively trivial pursuits. We can and should aim for more impactful applications that contribute to the betterment of human lives on a grand scale.

As we stand on the threshold of the Age of Agency, it is these questions that we must confront. Though they may seem philosophical or even abstract, they are essential to framing our approach to our shared future. The answers we find, or fail to find, will shape the trajectory of AI development and its impact on humanity. And in these answers, we may find the greatest opportunity of our age – the chance to blend the best of human and artificial intelligence for the good of all.

As we step back and consider all humanity, let us remember to do so with a light heart and an open mind. Yes, we must never be blind to the trials and tribulations that grip many sections of our world, but at the same time, let us not let the gravity of these issues weigh us down to the point of paralysis. This broad canvas upon which the human story is etched is also full of opportunities that lay strewn like stars in a night sky, waiting to be plucked by the dreamers, the doers, and the undeterred.

Indeed, when we talk about a world where demand far outstrips supply, it's not just a commentary on the areas of need but also an underlining of the vast ocean of opportunity ahead. We need more educators, innovators, and healers; we crave more music, art, and laughter; we need roofs over heads and nourishment for bodies; and, at the core, we seek the fulfilment of the human spirit.

In this era, where the world is but a global village and the gig economy brings prospects to our doorsteps, the term "opportunity" takes on a new dimension. You no longer have to be confined by geography or tradition. The modern-day entrepreneur is a global citizen with the potential to reach across continents and make a tangible difference.

This is not a plea for altruism or a rallying cry for charity – though noble those paths are. No, this book is about growth, business, and flourishing in an ever-evolving world. It is about harnessing your capacities and resources, both personal and organizational, to make a mark and prosper as you do so.

And what of capital, the lifeblood of enterprise? The modern era has shown us that ingenuity is no longer constrained by the purse. With an array of financial models, funding avenues, and innovative monetization strategies, the age-old adage, "Where there's a will, there's a way," has never been truer. The fetters that once bound dreams to capital constraints are loosening, and the only limitations are those of imagination and ambition.

So, let us cast our gaze further, let our visions fly unshackled, and let the winds of innovation and determination fill our sails. The horizon that stretches before us is vast and unexplored. But let us not be daunted. Let us be the explorers, the trailblazers, and the harbingers of a world where growth is not just personal but shared; where prosperity is not hoarded but sowed across fields of endless possibility.

In zooming out, we see not just the stark plight but also the vibrant potential of humanity. In this, every thread is an opportunity to weave a legacy of growth, innovation, and fulfilment. The horizon beckons; let us answer with bold hearts and unwavering steps.

Seeking to Understand

After a grand exploration of our world, it's time to rein in our wanderlust and turn inward for a moment. In the previous chapter, we delved deeply into the theoretical constructs of understanding our environment and our market. Now, in the heart of "The Real World," we have been immersing ourselves in the very fabric of human existence, reacquainting ourselves with the mundane and the miraculous alike. The objective of these experiences, both conceptual and practical, converge towards one critical point: the necessity of seeking to understand.

In Chapter 3, we discussed the pivotal role of observation, or as it is more commonly known, listening. Through this practice of quiet attentiveness, growth finds its fertile ground. Without it, we are navigating blindly, led astray by our own assumptions and biases. However, in an era marked by digitization and technological progress, the act of listening is increasingly becoming a lost art.

Our present reality is characterized by an overwhelming dependence on technology, where our senses are ensnared by the lure of the virtual world encapsulated in our handheld devices. This tether to the digital realm often leaves us disconnected from our physical surroundings and, more crucially, from each other. The irony is that as we increasingly rely on artificial intelligence, we risk becoming more artificial and less intelligent.

But this need not be our fate. The rise of AI doesn't necessarily spell the demise of human connection. On the contrary, it presents us with a powerful tool to understand our world better if only we use it wisely. Instead of becoming enthralled by our apps and gadgets, we can harness them as conduits to enhance our understanding of each other and our environment.

The data generated by social media platforms, online forums, and other digital channels can provide us with invaluable insights into the human condition. When analysed and interpreted correctly, this wealth of information can help us discern the underlying needs, desires, and aspirations of our fellow humans.

Armed with these insights, we can then steer our careers or design our products and services to better cater to these needs. Whether it's embarking on a large-scale project to address food scarcity in a foreign land or starting a small business venture in your local community, the cornerstone of success lies in attentive listening and understanding. In this Age of AI, our prosperity hinges on our capacity to maintain a keen sense of awareness, to understand the balance between humanity and technology, and to wield this understanding in our pursuit of growth.

Indeed, data collection is not a stand-alone task. It is a crucial part of the larger process of understanding. The knowledge gleaned from varied sources serves as a compass, guiding our decisions, shaping our strategies, and ensuring that our efforts align with the realities of our environment and the needs of our market. Here is why all these steps are integral:

Our world is rife with data waiting to be harnessed. It's in old invoices, client conversations, social media posts, and even in our casual conversations. While these pieces of information might seem random and disjointed, they are all clues leading us closer to understanding. What's the common thread tying our customers together? What are the nuances that shape their buying decisions? Why do they choose us, and how can we continue to serve them better?

The Age of Agency is characterized by a more active, informed, and discerning consumer. They aren't simply buying products or services, they are buying experiences, solutions, and values. As such, it's no longer sufficient to just push out marketing messages. Today, we need to engage, to resonate, to connect. We need to understand our market not just demographically, but psychographically as well.

This understanding is the cornerstone upon which *Basic Marketing* and *Reality in Advertising* methods are built. It is the bedrock upon which we can craft strategies that truly resonate. And more importantly, it empowers us to adapt, to pivot when necessary, and to continue growing amidst the changing tides of the market.

Understanding is also what allows us to maintain our connection to the world around us. In our increasingly digital age, it is easy to become detached, engrossed in our screens, and lost in the noise of endless data. But by grounding our data collection efforts in genuine care and interest for our fellow man, we not only keep ourselves grounded, but we also make our endeavours more impactful.

In the end, data collection isn't about hoarding information. It's about shedding light on the human experience, understanding the world in all its complexity, and leveraging this understanding to serve better, connect deeper, and succeed in the Age of Agency. The real world is a dynamic, complex, and vibrant space, and the more we strive to understand it, the more capable we become in navigating our way towards success.

Chapter 13

Rise with AI

IkigAI

We have recognized the boundless potential within each human being, navigated the realms of artificial intelligence, unpacked the concept of care, delved into marketing theories, and been jolted by the stark realities of the real world. Our journey has been both enlightening and disquieting. As we have ventured through these myriad realms, our steps have been shadowed by an ever-persistent question – a question that resonates with a new sense of urgency as we confront the Age of AI. What is the purpose of all this?

In Chapter 12, "The Real World," we were exposed to the raw and unvarnished condition of humanity at a global scale. The imbalances, the deprivations, and the boundless unmet needs painted a canvas that compelled us to reflect on the essence of our endeavours. What, then, should be the guiding force behind our actions? For what purpose should we harness the phenomenal capacities that AI and our innate human faculties afford us? Is there a greater, unified goal towards which our individual and collective efforts should strive?

As we venture into this final chapter, it's time to pivot. While Chapter 12 observed the human condition and our collective responsibilities from a macro, global standpoint, Chapter 13 shifts the focus inward onto the individual and business perspectives. How do we, as individuals or entities, find our place and purpose within this broader setting?

This is where the concept of "Ikigai" enters the stage. A Japanese term, "Ikigai," means "reason for being." It is the delicate balance at which your passions, talents, the needs of the world, and economic sustainability converge.

 DOI: 10.4324/9781032684895-17

It is the golden mean that promises fulfilment, contentment, and a sense of contribution.

Employing "Ikigai" as our guiding light, we will seek to harmonize our personal aspirations with the imperatives of the larger world. We will explore how individuals and businesses can find their unique purpose. This focal point resonates with their deepest values while also contributing positively to the global canvas we observed in Chapter 12.

As we set forth into this final chapter, let's pause and take stock of the journey thus far. We are about to connect the dots to see how the fabric woven by the preceding chapters takes on new textures and colours through the lens of "Ikigai." Prepare yourself for the crescendo as we awaken to the possibilities of rising with AI, not as mere beneficiaries of technological advancements but as torchbearers of purpose and agents of meaningful change.

First and foremost, it's important to understand that the Venn diagram that has become synonymous with Ikigai, showing an intersection point among four areas, doesn't accurately depict the traditional essence of Ikigai. This is, in fact, more of a Western interpretation. Ikigai, in its more authentic sense, is not necessarily a sweet spot where elements of your work life all harmoniously align for you to find purpose and financial success. For many, Ikigai is not even connected to economic status.

In this text, we are employing this unofficial "framework" only because it happens to be a useful tool to communicate certain aspects of finding purpose.

While there is no official "Ikigai framework," we can use this as a loose guide to illustrate some key points to consider when searching for one's meaning and purpose in life. For this reason, this text will not employ the typical Venn diagram approach. The Venn diagram implies a mathematically precise overlap across these four areas, which is too clinical for the rich and often non-linear journey of discovering purpose. Instead, we leave it to you, the reader, to engage with this material and reflect. Upon reflection, some ideas and insights may emerge. These emerging insights are what we are most interested in, as they are born from a personal and deeper understanding of one's own unique path to finding purpose.

Let's embark on an exploration of the four realms of Ikigai. As we delve into each of these realms, I encourage you to keep a notepad or digital note-taking tool close. Engage your curiosity and imagination, and note down the possible ideas and inspirations.

1. **That which you love**: love and passion are often the driving forces behind what we do. In the Age of AI, being more discerning and introspective about our passions is crucial. For instance, if you adore writing copy, let's peel back the layers. Is it the thrill of finding the perfect adjective, the art

of weaving emotions into words, or the satisfaction of delivering a message concisely? AI tools can help with grammar, and syntax, and even generate ideas, allowing you to focus on the nuance – the soul of your writing. With AI handling some logistics, your love can evolve into a more refined and focused passion.

2. **That which the world needs**: with AI taking over many mundane tasks, human creativity and problem-solving skills become even more valuable. Reflect on the broader challenges and needs presented in Chapter 12. Think globally, ponder about environmental sustainability, mental health, or education. Consider how technology can connect individuals from different cultures and how AI can be harnessed to address these global challenges. As AI continues to evolve, we must direct its application towards causes that uplift humanity.

3. **That which you can be paid for**: the digital age has revolutionized earning avenues. With AI at the helm, these avenues are being redefined yet again. Blockchain technologies like NFTs and cryptocurrencies are creating new value systems. Remote work, facilitated by AI-driven tools, is connecting talents with opportunities beyond borders. Additionally, AI can optimize your skills, thereby adding value to your work. For instance, if you are a designer, AI tools can hasten the prototyping phase, enabling you to focus on creativity and, potentially, earn more by taking on additional projects.

4. **That which you are good at**: proficiency is not just about what you can accomplish with your skills alone, it's also about how you can augment them with AI. For example, a lyricist with a talent for crafting emotive verses could use AI to find the perfect musical arrangement. A data analyst can leverage AI for faster data processing, focusing on interpretation and strategy. The synergy between your skills and AI can unlock potentials that were once thought unattainable.

As we reflect on the traditional Ikigai elements, it's essential to introduce an additional facet that aligns with the ever-evolving landscape of AI and technological advancements. This facet serves as both a reality check and an opportunity for personal evolution. Let's call this the fifth element of the IkigAI paradigm: "That which the future no longer needs from me."

5. **That which the future no longer needs from me**: as the Age of AI continues to accelerate, it's essential to acknowledge that AI may better execute certain tasks and responsibilities we once held. This is not a point for despair, but rather an invitation to reimagine our roles. For instance, a graphic designer or stock photographer needs to be mindful of tools like Midjourney and similar AI-driven design platforms that can produce images at a fraction of the time it would take a human.

Embracing this change doesn't mean relinquishing our purpose; instead, it involves pivoting and finding new avenues where our human touch is invaluable. The graphic designer, for example, could focus on more meaningful designs, brand storytelling, or consulting, where human creativity and strategic thinking remain unmatched.

By letting go of the tasks that AI can handle more efficiently, we free up our time and mental resources to explore more fulfilling areas less likely to be automated. This adaptation makes us invaluable and ensures that we are working within our passions and contributing meaningfully.

It is a humbling and empowering realization. It's about embracing the symbiosis between human talents and AI capabilities to forge a future that is not only efficient but also deeply harmonious with our truest selves and the needs of the world.

By integrating this fifth element into the traditional Ikigai model, the IkigAI paradigm becomes a more holistic and future-oriented framework. It encourages us not just to find our purpose but also to continually evolve with the times. It's about being fluid, adaptable, and open to the endless possibilities that arise when human ingenuity collaborates with the prowess of AI. This unique paradigm, tailored for the Age of AI, prepares us to thrive in a world that is as exciting as it is unpredictable.

Rising above the Noise

As we traverse through this age akin to a cacophony of sounds and stimuli, it's indispensable to acknowledge our position amidst it all. We've previously delved into the duality of discipline and distraction in Chapter 4, but here let's strip away the layers and peer into the day-to-day intricacies of our lives.

We exist in what can aptly be called "Distraction Central." A whirlwind of social media notifications, endless podcasts, a torrent of emails, binge-worthy Netflix shows, and an array of messaging apps that incessantly demand our attention. These are just the tip of the iceberg; the modern professional juggles a staggering number of inboxes and sources of information and entertainment.

What exacerbates this situation is the relentless influx of content that seems to echo and reinforce our existing beliefs and desires. Our feeds and inboxes are replete with messages that stoke the flames of instant gratification. Everyone seems to be achieving monumental success overnight, and we begin to wonder why we can't do the same. The culture of immediacy creates an illusion of urgency and success that is unattainable and dangerously myopic.

Let's be clear – ambition is a driving force we must harness. However, when ambition transforms into an obsession for overnight success, it blinds us to the long-term consequences and takes us further from our true purpose. The noise becomes so deafening that the whispers of our IkigAI get drowned.

Now, let's add AI to this mix. In the Age of AI, our exposure to content, messages, and distractions is amplified exponentially. The algorithms are relentless, and the barrage is ceaseless. AI surfaces the fissures in our resolve more starkly, leaving us vulnerable if we don't take decisive action.

This is the moment where we need to invoke and amalgamate the resolve from The Power of Personal Agency, as discussed in Chapter 2. It's a call to arms to rise above the noise and take flight, not sporadically, but with sustained momentum. William Hutchison Murray's quote shared in Chapter 2 serves as a powerful reminder and a torch in the fog. Our agency is not just about making choices; it is about making choices congruent with our purpose, our IkigAI. It's about making choices that carry us forward for the day and the years to come.

In the Age of AI, the stakes are higher; the distractions are louder, and the illusions more beguiling. Our armour needs to be impenetrable and our focus unwavering. Our compass needs to be calibrated not by the noise around us but by the deep-seated purpose within us.

Let's make it our mission to soar above the noise, with our gaze firmly set on the horizon shaped by our IkigAI. Through deliberate and conscious efforts, let's build bridges between the now and the future, between our daily actions and our ultimate purpose. In this Age, our Personal Agency is our shield and our sword. Let us wield them with dexterity, wisdom, and an unrelenting commitment to the path that is uniquely ours.

As we continue navigating through the cacophony, another facet of our pursuit requires scrutiny: the interpretation and, often, misinterpretation of "doing what you love." In a world that incessantly buzzes about following passions, a subtle undercurrent has morphed this adage into a precarious ideology.

The original sentiment behind "doing what you love" was meant to encourage aligning one's career and life with passions and interests. However, an unhealthy extension has emerged as "do only what you love, and ignore the rest." This deviation nudges us towards the realm of self-indulgence and sets unrealistic expectations.

Let's ponder upon the real-life implications of this. When entrepreneurs embark on a journey to build a business centred around their passion, they are often unprepared for the array of ancillary tasks that accompany the venture. For instance, a person passionate about making artisanal chocolates and turning it into a business will also have to deal with accounting, logistics, marketing, and customer service. Not all of these tasks might ignite the same passion as making chocolates, but they are essential cogs in the machine.

Similarly, a corporate professional who loves strategy formulation might have to engage in meticulous data gathering, something they might find tedious. Yet, this forms the backbone of the strategy they love to develop.

When the ideology of "doing only what you love" meets the potent catalyst of instant gratification, it creates a volatile concoction. It creates a mirage where success seems just an arm's length away, and anything that doesn't immediately satisfy is deemed unnecessary. The mundane and seemingly tedious tasks are ignored or hastily executed, leading to a shaky foundation upon which the dreams are built.

This precarious approach can explain the crumbling of many start-ups and personal ventures. The founders, fuelled by passion, often overlook or undermine the importance of the less glamorous tasks. They fail to recognize that passion, though a potent fuel, is not the sole ingredient for success.

Rising above the noise is not just about soaring high on the wings of passion; it's also about meticulously building the craft, bolt by bolt, even if some of those bolts don't shine as brightly. It's about acknowledging that not every step of the journey will be amidst roses; some will be across thorns. But those thorns are as much a part of the path as the roses.

In the Age of AI, where possibilities seem infinite, we must ground ourselves in realism and holistic diligence. We must embrace the entirety of our pursuits – the exciting and the mundane, the fulfilling and the tedious.

By embracing this more encompassing approach, we ensure that our flight is not just momentary but sustained; our foundations not just glittering, but rock solid. Let us build our paths with both fervour and meticulous attention, for in this harmony lies the true essence of rising above the noise.

As we bring this section, "Rising Above the Noise," to a close, it is imperative to underscore the criticality of listening to the market, albeit at the risk of repetition. In Chapter 11, the invaluable insights of E. Jerome McCarthy and Rosser Reeves shed light on aligning value propositions with the pulse of the market. Through an array of tools and methodologies, such as social media analysis and consumer feedback, we explored the art and science of gauging market needs and wants.

Here in this chapter, our IkigAI framework further accentuates the importance of understanding "That which the world needs" and "That which you can be paid for." Intriguingly, this insistence on market awareness dovetails into the larger narrative of rising above the noise. In an era bombarded with information, where data has been equated to the new oil, there arises an imperative to distinguish between genuine information and mere noise.

Now, you might ask: How do we reconcile the seemingly contradictory objectives of rising above the noise while actively seeking market data, especially in an age of information overload? The answer lies in discernment and precision.

Being attuned to market needs doesn't imply opening the floodgates to an unending stream of information. Instead, it calls for a more surgical approach to data collection. We must cultivate the acumen to discern between the relevant and the extraneous. It is essential to question our information sources and weigh the credibility and relevance of the data obtained.

One might utilize targeted surveys, expert interviews, or industry-specific reports, ensuring that the data collected is aligned with specific objectives. Tools such as analytics and AI algorithms can also be leveraged to sift through massive datasets and extract meaningful insights.

Being intentional in information sourcing implies actively choosing what to listen to and what to ignore. It means setting a boundary that filters out the cacophony, letting in only the symphony of relevant data. In this quest, let us not be mariners lost at sea, swayed by the currents of information. Instead, let us be skilled navigators, steering our ships with astute precision towards the shores of understanding.

Thus, as we seek to rise above the noise, let us carry the compass of discernment and the map of intentional data sourcing. This is not a dismissal of the imperative to listen, but rather an elevation of the art of listening – listening not only widely but wisely. In doing so, we find harmony in our navigation through the Age of AI, a balance between the abundance of information and the clarity of insight, between the whisperings of the market and the echoes of our IkigAI.

A Call to Action

As we approach the finale of this transformative journey through the book, we arrive at a juncture of reflection and awakening. Here, under the banner of "A Call to Action," we collectively recognize that the relentless cycle of the rat race must end here.

Readers, let us take a moment to ponder the gravity of this statement: the rat race ends here. If our lives are perpetually ensnared in the whirlwind of "making ends meet" or merely living for today's fleeting pleasures, we inadvertently place ourselves on a collision course with obsolescence in the Age of AI. Let it be unambiguously understood – this is an era when we must steadfastly maintain our position ahead of AI to remain the architects of our destinies rather than becoming mere pawns in the grand scheme of automation.

Let us harken back to the insights garnered in Chapter 2 – AI, as astoundingly capable as it may be in various facets, is inherently devoid of the humanistic capacity to conjure goals, foster intentions, or dream of a grandiose future.

This tapestry of ambition, dreams, and aspirations is singularly woven into the loom of human consciousness.

Now, here lies the crux. If we succumb to the monotony of mundane existence, we abdicate our singular domain to AI's mechanical and deterministic progression. Such abdication is not only a relinquishment of our distinctiveness but a surrender to potential redundancy in the very world we have constructed.

This is not an alarmist proclamation. Nor is it a harbinger of doom. Instead, it is an urgent call to action. This call resonates with our inherent vigour; it is a summons to our indomitable spirit. It urges us to reclaim our sanctum of dreams, aspirations, and goals and to wield them as the quintessential instruments in carving our place in the Age of AI.

We must remain vigilant, constantly aligning our humanistic faculties with the evolving landscape, ensuring that our uniqueness is preserved and amplified. We stand at the brink of an age that is as much about our human essence as it is about technological marvels. This is the moment – not just to be bystanders or mere participants – but to be pioneers and torchbearers.

This is our Call to Action. In the following pages, let us delve deeper into what this call means for each of us and how we can harness the full spectrum of our potential to craft a future that resonates with our deepest IkigAI.

In this evocative journey of human development and AI emerges an epiphany – AI is inadvertently guiding us towards the rediscovery of our own humanity. It is as though, through the mirrored reflection of artificial intelligence, our quintessential human traits are accentuated. This is the elevation, the ascent, that we speak of when we mention "Rise with AI." Our concern is not merely scaling technological heights but achieving an apotheosis of human spirit and potential.

Here, let us draw a line in the sand. Let us solemnly vow to ourselves and the generations to come. The rat race, the monotonous scamper in the conformity labyrinth ends here. As stewards of human potential, we will embrace the mantle of agency and forge ahead, casting away the fetters that once bound us to mediocrity. In the Age of Agency, we reclaim our power; we are no longer rats but visionaries, creators, and trailblazers.

Chapter 12 laid before us a world where humanity yearns for connection, purpose, and engagement. It beckons us to ask – why delay the realization of our potential as a society, waiting on artificial entities to attain fractions of human capability? We possess abundant human resources, pulsating with creativity, empathy, and ingenuity. Let us harness this reservoir not just for economic or technological gains but for the edification of the human spirit.

Let us employ AI as a catalyst, a facilitator in this grand design, ensuring that it is aligned to serve the higher purpose of human elevation. The human race craves acknowledgement, a sense of worth, and the profound affirmation that arises from contributing to something larger than oneself. It would be a travesty to deprive humanity of such enrichment.

This, then, is the moment to galvanize our communities, to inspire, and to champion the cause of inclusivity. Let's breathe life into the aspirations of our fellow beings and create channels for every individual to immerse themselves in the vivacity of life. Let us master AI, where our human ingenuity employs its analytical prowess. Together, they can create an unprecedented mark of progress that is not solely grounded in data and algorithms but is imbued with compassion, creativity, and purpose.

This is our call to rise. This is our moment to ensure that, as we march forward, we do so arm in arm with AI, but never at the cost of our soul's fire. We shall kindle this fire and light the path for humanity to ascend to its true potential.

And now, as we arrive at the culmination of this transformative journey, we turn the spotlight onto you, the individual, the reader whose eyes have traversed the pages and whose mind has imbibed the essence of this narrative. With fervour and intent, we ask: What is your role in this meeting point of evolution and progress? What does the world need from you? What do you bring to the table in this symphony of human potential and technological advancement?

Throughout this book, you have been invited to peer through the looking glass to oscillate between the realms of the external world and the depths of your innermost sanctum. The pendulum swings of reflections and introspections are an unceasing dialogue. The question that arises like a phoenix from the ashes of all that has been explored is: "What now?"

This is not a mere whimper or a sigh at the end of a chapter. This is an impassioned rallying cry, a call that must resonate. "What now?" should reverberate with such intensity that the very foundations of your convictions are shaken.

If this book has served as a catalyst, it must ignite a relentless state of enquiry within you. If, after turning the final page, your heart races with the inexorable need for transformation, for redefinition, then this book has achieved its purpose. Conversely, if complacency whispers in your ear and beckons you back into the comfort of routine and stagnation, we urge you to retrace your steps through these pages and challenge yourself to look deeper.

The manner in which you engage with your work, the world, and the individuals around you must metamorphose. The paradigms within which you navigate your career must be shattered and rebuilt with newfound wisdom. The lens through which you perceive your value and contributions must be refocused and sharpened.

This is not an end but a genesis. It is the commencement of a quest that is as boundless as the universe and as intimate as a heartbeat. As you close this book, may your soul be aflame with questions that lead you down untrodden paths, as vast as the oceans and as piercing as a star's light cutting through the night.

May you, intrepid explorer, seeker of truths and weaver of dreams, embark on your odyssey with a heart open to discovery and a spirit indomitable. The world awaits you, with its endless possibilities and its relentless challenges. This call to rise is not just a mere summons. It is an entreaty for you to grasp the mantle of your potential and soar with it.

Go forth with a spirit both curious and resolute. Godspeed on your journey. The world needs you; it always has.

Chapter 14

Conclusion

As we draw this journey to a close, let's pause to reflect upon the insights we've unravelled in *Age of Agency: Rise with AI*. This book, an actionable blueprint, serves as an urgent alert to a rapidly evolving AI landscape. AI, no longer a distant marvel, now entwines with our daily realities. Our route through the preceding chapters has been deliberately laid out, transitioning from understanding our intrinsic human strengths to leveraging the help of AI to the irreplaceable essence of human connection and care in a digitized world. Here, in our conclusion, we aim to distil and reiterate some salient takeaways.

Part 1: Master Your Own Agency

This part underscored a significant point: our unparalleled human potential is our mainstay in an AI-dominated environment. The capabilities we need to hone, bet on, and showcase more prominently – namely observation, creativity, and resourcefulness – are the bedrock of our strength. These are not just attributes but essential tools to ensure that, in the face of AI's advances, we remain not just relevant but also influential.

Part 2: Master AI

In the second part, we tackled AI not as an overwhelming force but as a tool, an ally. The core message was clear: AI is a force multiplier, but only if we understand its capabilities and limitations. The challenge is to ensure that AI serves

 DOI: 10.4324/9781032684895-18

us, amplifying our efforts where they matter most, rather than relegating us to mere spectators.

Part 3: Develop Care

Transitioning to customer interactions, the third part highlighted a salient truth: in the AI era, genuine care is not a luxury – it's a necessity. Operational efficiency, powered by AI, is now a given. The true differentiator? Infusing humanity into every digital interaction, ensuring that every touchpoint echoes with authentic care and building trust and loyalty in the process.

Part 4: Understand Humanity

The fourth part brought forth an essential reminder: amidst the proliferation of AI-generated content, our humanity remains irreplaceable. No matter how advanced our digital tools become, the tangible world, driven by human needs and desires, is where the true value lies. Our strategies and actions must always prioritize this human element, offering value deeply rooted in human-centric service.

Armed with the wisdom from this book, the call to action is clear. In the current era, complacency is our greatest adversary. With agency in one hand and AI in the other, we possess the tools not just to survive, but to shape the Age of Agency. The time to act is now, for in this transformative era, standing still is the only real danger.

We must remember that our roles go beyond passive observers; we are dynamic actors, catalysts of change, and builders of bridges between technology and humanity. The Age of Agency is one that we traverse and actively shape. Through the mastery of our agency, the skilful utilization of AI, the nurturing of care, and an unwavering focus on humanity, we build a world that is technologically advanced yet deeply anchored in the values that define our humanness.

In a nutshell, the *Age of Agency: Rise with AI* offers a roadmap. As AI continues its relentless march forward, this book serves as a guide, emphasizing that our most potent weapon in this era is the combined force of our human faculties and an in-depth understanding of the tools at our disposal. The ball is now in our court: equipped with this knowledge, the onus is on us to act, shape, and define our destiny in the Age of AI.

Index

Printed in the United States
by Baker & Taylor Publisher Services